THE PRIVATE LIFE OF THE SOVIET ELITE

THE PRIVATE LIFE OF THE SOVIET ELITE

Ilya Zemtsov

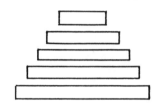

Crane Russak • New York

The Private Life of the Soviet Elite

Published in the United States by
Crane, Russak & Company, Inc.
3 East 44th Street
New York, NY 10017

Copyright © 1985 Crane, Russak & Company, Inc.

Library of Congress Cataloging in Publication Data

Zemtsov, Ilya,
The private life of the Soviet elite.

Bibliography: p.
1. Elite (Social sciences)—Soviet Union.
2. Social classes—Soviet Union. I. Title.
HN530.Z9E49   1985   305.5'2'0947   85-7805
ISBN 0-8448-1491-1 (pbk.)

Printed in the United States of America

Contents

Preface
Material Wealth and Spiritual Poverty of the Soviet Elite

In critiques of the theory and practice of communism as brought about by the communist state, the emphasis often falls on the betrayal of the promise of equality. The emergence of a "new class" and of a communist aristocracy is then invariably cited as evidence of this betrayal.

In journalistic or academic writings on the communist state, in particular on the USSR, much attention is paid to the luxuries that the elite, especially the ruling oligarchy, enjoys thanks to lavish privileges. Compared to the standard literature on the subject, Professor Ilya Zemtsov's book abounds in descriptive details of the elite's everyday life, in addition to providing a neat analysis of the mechanisms undergirding the formation of an oligarchy, its use of power for self-perpetuation, and its dispensation of power and concomitant benefits to other social groups. In this wealth redistribution system one's eligibility for any privileges depends on one's hierarchical rank, on that rank's distance from the top of the hierarchy, and on one's servility and sycophancy toward the top elite, or the "partocracy."

The Soviet state does supply the citizens with some basic goods and services, often cheaply, sometimes even for free. But, as Zemtsov shows, the gap between the populace and the elite is enormous, even if not immediately noticeable. In the midst of general poverty, the ruling class lives with material comforts reminiscent of those of the nobility of the *anciens régimes* in Europe and tsarist Russia or the *nouveau riche* robber barons in America and other industrialized countries.

The author shows how this system and its economy work: we are told how the black markets become bureaucratized and how this process serves the interests of the elite. We learn about the emergence of a pyramid of subelites, which vary in their access not only to power, but also to scarce consumer goods and services, with even the lowest ranking subelite consuming far more than the ordinary citizens. The communist *dolce vita* varies, therefore, in both standard and style, again depending on the distance of its given practitioner from the partocracy. At the same time, all segments of the elite distance themselves from their own rhetoric of equality and hard work and from the daily lives of the citizenry they help to exploit and keep in poverty.

Zemtsov tells a great deal about the process of recruitment to the elite ranks. The main criteria used in this process are continuously tested loyalty and obedience, but there are other criteria as well, such as being of Slavic extraction. In some sectors talent, organizational skills, or other traits of merit can count also. But ultimately, everything depends on nomenclatura, which arbitrarily assigns power along with the right to enjoy special access to scarce goods and services and the right to pass these benefits to others.

Thus, in the USSR a facade of cohesiveness is presented to outsiders while inside it is a "dog-eat-dog" world. Solidarity is needed to protect the power and privileges of those who have made it to the top, but to make their power and privileges truly secure, it has been necessary to constitute the elite as a hereditary class. This is achieved by creating homogeneity through the development of networks of family relations, i.e., a system of nepotism by endogamy and the enrolling of the elite's offspring in special schools providing high-quality education. In this way high living standards are secured for those sons and daughters of the elite who may, for whatever reasons, shun political careers in favor of academic or artistic ones. Like past aristocracies and nobilities, all Soviet elites, and in particular the partocracy, tend to accumulate, use, and delegate status signs and symbols, chiefly in the form of varying levels of conspicuous consumption.

The ensuing life styles of the Soviet elite, especially as they relate to the use of leisure time, provide no mean gratification. Zemtsov's descriptions of these life styles form some of the most fascinating parts of his study. The functions of the arrangements made for the elite are not difficult to define. First, in a system of oppression, exploitation, and enforced deprivation, the rulers must secure compliance through a modicum of legitimacy won by grants and denials of privileges and other rewards. Second, the system helps ensure loyalty to the central authority of the ruling class by every individual, group, and organization, including the nations constituted as the various Soviet republics. Third, in the face of overall inefficiency, rewards and privileges obtainable under this system minimize bottlenecks in the areas of production, supply, distribution, and services, as they offer the people a sense of hope for a bit of material comfort in the midst of economic deprivation.

And what about the democratic ideal? It is important to realize that this ideal has never been particularly pronounced in communist ideology. True, the state has proclaimed itself "democratic." But this lip service to the tenets of democracy reveals a paradox within Soviet society. The pseudo-democratic rituals of their elections actually constitute a refutation of Marxism. Reality no longer determines ideology, rather, it is ideology that determines reality. The main conclusion emerging from Zemtsov's study is that the ruling elite creates economic, social, and political conditions that Marxist theory perceives as prerevolutionary, but that revolution is precluded by the intimidation and power to dispense privileges exercised by the elite and by the wealth and luxury enjoyed by the few who prove truly loyal.

To this state of affairs individuals can adjust by retreating into apathy, inaction, or alcoholism; however, there also is another form of behavior that typifies the new Russian personality: the mask of compliance. Others, endowed with more enterprising spirits, may develop more "innovative" adaptations through engagement in criminal pursuits.

The connections between the described Soviet social structure and crime are evident, and several specific criminal developments can be observed. First and foremost, a complex system of a "second" economy for scarce goods and services appears that is based on black markets fueled in part by rationing but mainly by inefficiency. For all the corruption that this underground economy generates, it allows each segment of the social structure to acquire needed goods and services. In each section of the economy an entire network of employee theft, embezzlement, extortion, fraud, and corruption is thus bound to evolve. White-collar crime becomes organized crime. This explains, at least in part, why the inefficiency of official economic and public service institutions is tolerated and even sustained in the USSR, where the black market economy works quite efficiently and with precision.

The underground economy has given rise to a new class of criminals who mediate among the producers, distributors, consumers and other role performers in the economic system. They are "fences" of goods and services illegally obtained. These new "capitalists" maintain close contacts with all the segments of the communist elite class, providing the latter with all the requisites for luxurious and ostentatious life styles. The wealth thus accumulated is then used by subelites to bribe their or their children's way into special schools and institutions. In contrast, the lower classes have only two options if they want to maintain or raise their living standard even a little: employee theft or embezzlement. Some content themselves with ordinary theft or robbery.

The pervasive corruption in Soviet society also taints the medical, educational, and academic institutions. The official explanations of this can be quite facetious, as corruption is attributed to the "remnants of the capitalist system," to educational negligence, or to imitation of the West. The author's explanation of the criminal implications of the Soviet stratification system is Mertonian, referring to the gap between the goals and the means. Whenever goals are pursued by legitimate means, either the former are found to be unrealistic or the latter are found to be inadequate. The resultant deprivation acts as an incentive to resort to illegitimate means. Particularly fascinating are Zemtsov's descriptions of the periodic outbursts of moral purification, the crusades against corruption. The very fact that such campaigns are intermittent proves that they fail to achieve their purpose. Illegality is too entrenched in the social and economic system to be dealt with by such sporadic efforts to stamp it out. Actually, these efforts are largely symbolic in nature, as they help to maintain the facade of a "pure" core of the developed socialist society.

The scope of corruption in the non-Slavic republics of the USSR reflects the aspiration to close the perceived gap in standard of living between the non-Slavic population and the poor Slavic one. But the entrenchment of the corrupt underground economy is also reflected in character and personality formation. The typical *Homo Sovieticus* personality is unscrupulous and guileful under the mask of blind obedience to authority. The spread of such a character pattern contributes to the perpetuation of the entire sordid system. On the whole, however, the future of this system is only speculation. The author formulates such speculations in the form of scenarios of possible change that are interesting but not necessarily probable. Their low probability reflects Zemtsov's skepticism about the likelihood of change in a system that appears to be so well entrenched. Certainly, the system could also be abolished by a revolution, but this again is a remote possibility under the conditions of the monopoly of violence and threats of violence in the hands of the ruling class, a monopoly that seems all too sufficient for eliciting compliance.

In sum, one of the chief merits of the book is the plasticity of Zemtsov's descriptions as he makes the various elites and subelites come alive for the reader by emphasizing their private lives as well as the standards, tastes, and aspirations that they pursue daily. The same plasticity characterizes his descriptions of the workings of the system and the spiritual, social, and moral values that animate it.

The inescapable conclusion from Zemtsov's work is that "developed," "mature," and "real" socialism (labels that imply the existence of some "undeveloped," "immature," and "unreal" socialism) is perfectly possible in the USSR—but not for the entire society, merely for the elite. Thus, the Soviet society revealed by the pages of the profound and instructive book of Professor Zemtsov is a society for the chosen few.

Professor Menachem Amir

Director of the Institute of Criminology
Hebrew University of Jerusalem

Acknowledgments

We wish to express our sincere appreciation to the minister of science and development of the State of Israel and the staff of the ministry for their continued support of the International Research Center on Contemporary Society and this publication in particular.

We are witness in Soviet society to the materialization of ideology, the abstract (Marxist) idea becoming embodied in concrete government. Communist ideology is taking root and establishing itself in the life of a great country, and in the process is crushing an extraordinary people. Herein lies tragedy: the people wanted to master an idea, but the idea has mastered the people.

Chapter 1

The Rich and the Poor

In the USSR, privileges are valued more than money. They are legitimized by the party and are not subject to taxation.

A person in the Soviet Union for the first time need not ask where the Committee of the Communist Party is located. All he has to do is to find the main street in the center of any town. There he will find the inevitable statue of Lenin pointing, directing, looking boldly into the future; nearby is the pretentious, pompous, and tasteless building of the party corporate offices. This feature of the Soviet cityscape is not fortuitous; it is the symbolic expression of the spirit of contemporary Russia, whose religion is communist ideology and whose all-powerful and ruling priests are the party bureaucrats.

A day in the USSR begins in these buildings, so unsuited to the rhythm of contemporary life, and ends in perfect conformity with the will and wishes of those who inhabit them. The vast majority of the people, the citizens of this great and powerful country, have nothing but a few personal possessions, yet the party leaders—arrogant partocrats, the top elite of a new Communist class who have illicitly accumulated incredible wealth— allocate the resources of the country in their own self-interest, for their own gain. Even if Russia had been under the heel of conquerors for centuries, it is doubtful that the people could have been so cruelly and thoroughly robbed, a people which only sixty years ago were 80 percent small peasants.[1]

In the program of the Communist Party the Soviet people were promised that the 1970s would be a time of prosperity. In the early 1980s it has been ascertained that the standard of living in the USSR occupies twenty-fifth place compared with other countries, that the standard of living in Russia is down to 46 percent of what it was in 1917, and that according to national income per capita it is still further down the list, in twenty-eighth place. But even these facts do not present a complete picture of the impoverishment of the working masses in Soviet society. Some 36 percent of the total government wage fund in 1981 was allocated among 10 percent of the population: to 3 percent of the workers in the Soviet party apparatus, to 2.3 percent of the regular party workers and military workers, to 2.1 percent of the scientific workers, and to 2.6 percent of the managers of industry and of agriculture. To this same 10 percent went 83 percent of the private automobiles, 86 percent of the government summer homes, and 64 percent of the cooperative apartments. And in 1982 alone the same 10 percent received 48 percent of all the passes to sanatoriums and resorts and 33 percent of the newly constructed housing.

While for 1980 the official minimum income level per month per person in the USSR was 51 rubles 30 kopecks, income per person in the families of the Soviet elite was as follows: party officials, 168 rubles; regular military personnel, 153 rubles; scientific workers, 142 rubles; managers of industry and agriculture, 133 rubles. If the amount of remuneration for labor is the criterion for social usefulness, then the people most necessary to the country are the party workers. They are less than 2 percent of all the workers in the country, but they receive 8.1 percent of the total wages paid.[2] Nevertheless, in terms of stress and qualifications, the social value of the party functionary is clearly inferior to engineering or education work, and in terms of output it cannot be compared with that of a scientist or even a skilled worker. Moreover, according to sociological studies conducted in the USSR, party bureaucrats read little—32 percent less than engineers, 49 percent less than teachers, 71 percent less than scientists. They attend the theater and concerts less frequently than engineers (by 43 percent), than teachers (by 76 percent), than scientists (by 51 percent). At the same time, they are the solid majority among the habitués of hockey and soccer matches—more than engineers by 29 percent, more than teachers by 39 percent, more than scientists by 78 percent. The qualitative parameters of their personality are also revealing. Among Moscow party workers, 32 percent are highly nervous and not sufficiently communicative, 28 percent lack sufficient knowledge in their spheres of authority, and 12.9 percent suffer from psychological syndromes.[3]

Still, one should not assume that Soviet party officials receive more than they are worth: they are paid by a government that does not overpay anyone. They are rewarded not for their labor and not for the usefulness of their activities, their intellect, their talents, or their training, but for their services and primarily for their loyalty to the regime. Moreover, the closer they are to the mechanisms of power, the greater their potential influence and the more generously their activities are compensated. Conversely, the further a social stratum is from the control levers of government, the less its influence on policy and the lower its salary. Here too the social usefulness or value of the labor performed is of no significance.

The annual earnings of nearly 30 percent of the families in the USSR do not exceed 1,600 rubles (approximately 32 rubles per month per person). These are primarily collective farmers and, in part, state farm workers. This group is at the very bottom of the social pyramid. It has fewer rights and less protection than others, and consequently earns less than others.[4]

The family income of factory workers, who constitute 27 percent of the population, is somewhat higher—about 2,300–2,400 rubles annually. The monthly per capita income in 59 percent of workers' families (44 rubles) is below the minimum living standard; for 22 percent of the families it hovers at that level, and for only 19 percent of the families does it exceed it somewhat (53–57 rubles).

The extremely low wage scale of workers and peasants in the USSR is a result of the monopolization of power and property by the new Communist ruling class. In the Soviet Union there is no labor market. There is only one employer—the partocracy—and the workers are forced to sell their labor on the terms it finds profitable and convenient. In the USSR there is no relation between workers' wages and the profit the government reaps from their labor. However, there are political and economic factors that place a limit on the exploitation of the workers.

The workers and peasants, on which the efficiency and stability of the state depend and on which, consequently, the well-being of the dominant party nomenclatura (see Chapter 3) also depends, have little interest in their work. Even more than other strata, the workers and peasants have no desire to master or serve complicated modern technology. As a result, production is of low quality, productivity remains low, equipment quickly runs down, and technological progress is impeded. To counter this, the regime is forced to allot minimum attention to improving the working conditions of the laborers and the living conditions of rural inhabitants. This constitutes an objective constraint on the communist system's exploitation of the workers, but needless to say, the workers' wages are also constrained. Their upper limit is contingent on the advantage of the Soviet ruling class.

Another factor limiting exploitation is fear. The Soviet leadership's fear of the working masses is fed not only by the hopelessness of the situation of the masses, which incites them to insubordination and passive resistance to the authorities, but also by communist ideology itself, which is accustomed to seeing in the impoverished proletariat (the working class in the USSR is even poorer than it was under the czars) and the landless peasantry (the Soviet collective farm peasantry is completely propertyless) a dynamic, revolutionary force with great capacity for organization.

The yearly income of 19 percent of Soviet families—engineering-technical workers, lower government and bank workers, economic planners, and certain categories of trade workers—is approximately 2,500 rubles, about the same as in workers' families. In these families, however, the monthly income per person is somewhat higher (indicating smaller family size): 49–59 rubles.

The real annual income per family of another 14 percent of the population (primarily not involved in production—teachers, lawyers, doctors) approaches the income of workers or falls below it: 2,250–2,400 rubles. The wage scale of this category of the Soviet population is related to its social influence. The members of the so-called free professions in the USSR are extremely isolated from each other and are wholly dependent on the authorities, who allot them only the smallest subsistence income.[5]

The general figures on the incomes of the Soviet citizenry are even lower if one considers the fact that 44 percent of people retired because of age or infirmity have an income below the minimum living standard.[6] At the same time, the ruling class and the segment of the middle class that serves it, comprising the remaining 10 percent of the working population, receive an income per person 250–300 percent higher than the minimum living standard and live comfortably, even affluently.

The income statistics to which we have referred cast doubt on the official Soviet statement that workers earn 151 rubles per month.[7]* This, of course, is an average, as the Soviet sources invariably concede, or rather emphasize, and averages can conceal wide differences among those contributing to them. If one were to average the earnings of a collective farmer (60–70 rubles a month) with that of a Soviet officer (240–260 rubles a month), one would indeed arrive at close to 151 rubles. Add instead to the earnings of the collective farmer the salary of a top official of a regional committee (400 rubles), and the "average" wages of two Soviet workers would be significantly higher. Workers' income increases even more when the earnings of a collective farmer or teacher are combined with the salary of a minister, general, or people's artist. But returning to the official figure of 151 rubles, it should be noted that this monthly wage is significantly lower than what *unemployed* West German or Swedish workers receive.

In the USSR the unemployed do not receive any compensation, and it should be noted that there are unemployed persons. Approximately 10 million people change work annually[8]—in official Soviet jargon this is euphemistically called "personnel flow." If it is assumed that these personnel spend about one

---

*By 1981 this figure had risen insignificantly—to 157 rubles.

month seeking new employment and the annual figures are re-computed accordingly, there are more unemployed in the USSR than there are in England or France.

It is true that the Communist regime does provide an elementary minimum of social protection. It offers everyone a job, but the guaranteed right to work has led to the creation of a million fictitious work openings and to the bureaucratization of the industrial process. The government demands minimal rents for apartments, perhaps the lowest in the world, but each person receives on the average 5–6 square meters, depending on the city of residence, and even this norm is hardly guaranteed. Such is the face of Soviet "rights."

The economic development of the USSR continually lags behind that of the United States. This gap is constantly increasing in favor of the United States; the comparative ratio of their present rates of development is approximately 1 to 3.5.[9] According to the next five-year plan, by 1990 the USSR will reach only three-fourths of the national income promised to Soviet society fifteen years ago.[10] Furthermore, it is doubtful that even this level of economic development will be attained by the USSR: the annual increase in production declines each year, and labor productivity is not increasing. The crisis continues to worsen. Yet radical economic changes will inevitably entail rapid social and political changes greater than the current Soviet bureaucracy can withstand. The threat to the ruling class will intensify even further as soon as the masses begin to demand the rights promised them in the new Soviet constitution: workers demanding sharing of profits; peasants demanding the right to dispose of lands; nationalities demanding genuine independence.

Thus, according to Marxist theory, political conditions in the USSR are ripe for revolution: the relations of production are hindering the development of the forces of production, and the nomenclatura has created its gravediggers in the persons of the downtrodden workers. But there is as yet no revolutionary crisis in the USSR, and its eruption cannot be predicted. Processes within Soviet society cannot be forecast on the basis of social variables alone. For analysis of Soviet social structure, no less important are the psychological variables affecting the actions of the Soviet political leadership. This factor is in many respects concealed from view, a mystery. And so, when such a crisis will erupt, or for how long the society will remain stagnant and the people will endure degradation, oppression, and exploitation, are questions without answers. At the present there are no mass arrests and oppression as under Stalin, but there is constant systematic anxiety. Women have difficulty coping with work both in the home and at their place of employment; youth have difficulty with absurd school programs; men have the problem of earning additional income on the side or on the black market. All are involved in the exhausting struggle for survival. The Soviet authorities have lost their calm and sense of stability. They suffer from powerlessness and fear.

If under these circumstances there is still no spontaneous eruption, no dramatic mass protest, it is only because both would immediately be drowned in blood and cruelly repressed. It is no easy matter to display heroism in a totalitarian system, where a coercive apparatus penetrates every level of existence. To express one's protest via vodka is simpler and less dangerous. The people drink—from necessity, from habit—to forget.[11]

A person who does not possess the property an income can bring, who does not receive the profit that would allow him to acquire significant savings and satisfy the most essential spiritual and material needs, can be considered a deprived person. He may be energetic, talented, and educated, but he is deprived. According to this understanding, 90 percent of the population of the USSR is poor, although by no means do all lack the means of existence or live in poverty. But if any one of them were to lose his employment for even a month he would be totally ruined. And this, to a greater degree than injustice and force, fear and coercion, leads to utter obedience.

An important digression must be made here to note that in the beginning of the 1960s, Khrushchev, the first secretary of the Central Committee of the Soviet Communist Party, triumphantly promised that within the lifetime of the present generation the Soviet Union would build communism. Khrushchev meant that the standard of living, measured in the per capita production of goods and products, would catch up with and surpass the United

States. Twenty years later it is interesting to see how the promise
of the Communist leader was realized. Tables 1 and 2 compare
the amount of working time that must be spent in both countries
to acquire essential foodstuffs and consumer goods. The tables
make it clear that while the Soviet consumer has broad opportunities for eating his fill of bread and potatoes, everything else is
substantially less accessible to him than it is to a worker in the
United States. This picture does not do credit to "the first proletarian government in the world." The Communists force workers to work significantly longer than Western workers in order to
acquire the most essential goods and products. The advantages
of Soviet socialism in comparison with the West are unmistak-
able. Soviet citizens are better off only when it comes to purchasing movie theater tickets (communism has implemented the
slogan "Entertainment instead of bread") and public transportation (as if to corroborate the view of Lenin and Marx that "all
roads lead to communism").

The hopelessness of the existence of the worker in the USSR
is aggravated by the fact that the Soviet citizen cannot buy many
essential food products and consumer goods at the heavily sub-
sidized prices and is forced to pay exorbitant prices for them at
the open market or under the counter.[12]

According to the constitution, medical services in the USSR
are free, but to obtain a place in a hospital one must pay heavily;
bribes amount to from 100 percent to 300 percent of the monthly

Table 1
Working Time Spent to Acquire Essential Foodstuffs in the
United States and the USSR

	USA	USSR
lb. white bread	10 min.	9 min.
lb. meat	16 min.	94 min.
lb. sugar	4 min.	29 min.
liter milk	7 min.	21 min.
doz. eggs	12 min.	116 min.
lb. fish	20 min.	40 min.
lb. potatoes	4 min.	3 min.

Table 2
Working Time Spent to Acquire Consumer Goods in the
United States and the USSR

	USA	USSR
Man's suit	25 hrs.	106 hrs.
Pair of nylon stockings	16 min.	144 min.
Bar of toilet soap	5 min.	72 min.
20 cigarettes	10 min.	24 min.
Color television	47 hrs.	160 hrs.
100-watt lightbulb	8 min.	30 min.
10 gallons gasoline	91 min.	190 min.
Bus ticket	6 min.	4 min.
Postage stamp	2 min.	3 min.
Movie theater ticket	41 min.	30 min.
Haircut	51 min.	30 min.

salary of a skilled worker.[13] The myth of free and generally available medical help in the USSR is propaganda directed toward the uninformed Western public. After having physically destroyed tens of millions of its citizens, the Communist regime is attempting to demonstrate to world public opinion its concern for the health of its people. Under the system of so-called free medical service, the Soviet citizen must not only pay for a place in the hospital but in the hospital itself must buy his meals, because the miserable hospital ration allotted him is stolen, and must pay bribes if he wants care and medicines, because the hospital pharmacies do not stock the latest drugs.

It is impossible for simple working people to receive a free pass to a rest home or sanatorium *each year*. Such a pass in fact costs twice its nominal value since bribes are required to obtain one. As for apartments, in sixty to seventy cases out of a hundred they are earmarked only for those who have the money to pay bribes: the amount of the bribe is two to three times a worker's annual salary. Bribes are necessary not only for an apartment in a government building but also for legitimating (registering in the regional executive committee) a clay hut built by a family in its spare time; such an operation costs up to 1,000 rubles. But do-it-yourself housing, built by primitive methods, does not last long and quickly falls into disrepair. There are dirt, unpleasant odors, health hazards. When epidemics begin the government is forced to resettle the family, but here too bribes are essential. The "fee" of the regional executive committee is 500 to 1,000 rubles. To pay less is impossible, for the money has to be divided between committee and other officials.[14]

The workers, robbed by the government, do not remain honest in relation to that government and, trying somehow to make ends meet, become involved in all sorts of speculation, extortion, and swindles. While the "take" on the part of the workers is not large—how much can be stolen from a factory or swiped from a collective farm?—the bigwigs of large enterprises reach their hands into government banks, depositories, and storehouses and skim off millions. The authorities are apparently unharmed by these attempts to redistribute what has been stolen in the first place.

The corruption runs into millions of rubles, encompassing industrial enterprises and restaurants and penetrating government establishments. On one occasion, in 1960, the editor-in-chief of *Izvestiya* attempted to take up the challenge. This was not simply the editor-in-chief of the central government newspaper, but also the chairman of the Commission of the Supreme Soviet on Foreign Affairs, Aleksei Adzhubei, son-in-law of Khrushchev. Special investigators for extraordinary cases from the prosecutor's office of the USSR were immediately dispatched to Krasnodar, a town in central Russia apparently fully controlled by organized crime. The task of the investigators was to apprehend and punish the guilty parties. In Krasnodar the investigators sent to restore Soviet legality and socialist order were arrested and severely beaten. Adzhubei complained to the Politburo, which in response ordered the inquest stopped and the investigators returned. The disgraced Adzhubei was left to guess whether Politburo member Polyansky, who had come to Krasnodar's defense, was a member of the "mafia" or simply looked after its interests.[15]

But in the USSR it is not only city authorities who are involved in such illegal business activities. The scale of black market business can well extend over whole republics. For a period of twenty years (from the 1960s to the 1980s) the party leaderships of Georgia and Azerbaijan were twice arrested and totally replaced.[16]

The 1970s and early 1980s introduced new hues to the picture of criminal goings-on in the USSR. In one case, a group of "illegal" businessmen were arrested in one of the Soviet republics. In the course of the investigation and inquest it became known that the wife of the first secretary of the Central Committee of the republic was involved in suspect activities. It became necessary to turn the investigation on her. The minister of internal affairs requested permission from the first secretary of the Central Committee. His request was refused. Next he asked the attorney general of the USSR, also without success. Quite despairing, he managed to arrange a meeting with the General Secretary of the Central Committee of the Communist Party of the Soviet Union (CPSU). The result was totally unexpected: a decree was issued to remove the first secretary of the Central Committee of the republic. In a southern Soviet republic there began a "month's campaign of Soviet legality."[17] An example is appropriate here: A person was killed in a highway accident. No charges were brought against the guilty party. This cost him thirteen thousand rubles, which the police investigator and the government prosecutor divided between them.[18]

Those who have power in the USSR take their bribes not only in money but also in kind. In one southern republic it came to light that the furniture, rugs, and crystal of the third secretary were identical to the furnishings of one of the managers of a textile trust arrested for the theft of millions. "Presents"—bribes—had obviously been received by the third man in the republic.[19] The way of life of the Soviet elite is a strictly guarded government secret, but in this instance something had gone awry. It became necessary to remove the secretary of the Central Committee of the republic. During a search of the apartment of the regional prosecutor of another republic, thirty-four rugs, mountains of crystal, gold coins, and rolls of hundreds of meters of silk were found. This unlucky "guardian of justice" was guilty of demanding a "cut" of the bribes given the director of a pedagogical college from those who wished to study in the college.[20]

From reading Soviet newspapers, it is not easy to determine how deeply the criminal "mafia" has penetrated governing circles in Soviet society. One gets the impression that it is more appropriate to speak not about penetration but about fusion of the two worlds: power and organized crime. One head of an arts institute was, naturally, a Communist. He acquired tens of thousands of rubles for "dead souls," people who never worked at the institute. He also used tens of thousands of the institute's rubles to pay teachers. As one music teacher related, "The director of the music college gave me empty examination forms and demanded that I assign grades according to his wishes to applicants I had never seen." He continued, "We assigned good grades even when the applicant could not play at all." Examination cribs were also sold, the purchase price depending on the grades. The price of a crib also depended on the applicant's ability to pay: a kindergarten teacher paid 300 rubles, a factory bookkeeper paid 500 rubles, a locksmith paid 600 rubles, and so on. The cribs were sold not only for cash but also for favors and services the applicant could render the teacher. "Remember, fulfill your duty and keep silent," the director of the college demanded from a subordinate, as the regional authorities had demanded from him. One might ask whether it is possible to inculcate principles by means of unscrupulousness. Apparently it is, if unscrupulousness itself has become a principle. This the director of the music college well knew from the experience he had already accrued as former head of the cultural section of a regional executive committee.

The motives for corruption are not so easily explained. Thus one driver could not give a sensible account of what he had done with twenty sacks of wheat. He could not relate that he had taken them to sell so that the chairman of the collective farm could make payment to the regional committee of the party for lowering the plan figures, or—equally possible—to someone in the regional machinery office in order to receive on time some essential piece of harvesting equipment. And thus the poor

driver was left to wiggle out of his predicament, however uncon-
vincingly, as if he had taken it all for himself, being so gluttonous
that he devoured grain by the kilo.[21] False reporting, embezzlement, and bribery have penetrated (and paralyzed) all aspects of
Soviet society. The extent of this penetration can be gauged from
the following excerpt from proceedings of the Plenum of the
Central Committee of Uzbekistan in 1984: "Communist leaders
who have lost all shame and morality had handsome apartments
in the city, but in addition to them owned houses and two or
three cars. Only recently were their villas taken away from
them." Many nomenclatura functionaries have been removed
from their posts and subjected to prosecution in a move calculated to teach others a lesson.

In the spring and summer of 1984 the newspapers of Uzbekistan depicted the realities of overt corruption which engulfed the
republic's elite, manifesting itself in nepotism, bribery, embezzlement, and abuse of office. Although no one was charged with
political crimes, many, including ministers and secretaries of
party provincial committees, were fired. Had the first secretary
of the Communist Party of Uzbekistan, Sharif Rashidov, remained alive, he might also have lost his post, just as ten years
previously this had happened to the rulers of Azerbaijan and
Georgia. But it is also possible that had Rashidov been alive he
would have been capable of using his authority effectively to
stem the tide of press exposés against his cronies (after all, he
had been kingpin in the republic for almost a quarter of a century).

Exposures in the Soviet press of moral degradation (referred
to as the "degeneration of ruling cadres") can be taken as an
indication of the dissatisfaction of the Chernenko leadership
with the results of communist education and indoctrination. This
explains why in recent Soviet press commentaries scholars and
university professors have increasingly been singled out for criticism. For example, the head of the Department of Zoology of
Kirghiz State University, Professor A. T. Toktosunov, was lam-
basted for his discovery of a new way of making a fast ruble. He
and his associates had used materials available to them in a
museum they were in charge of to provide stuffed animals for

sale. In the process they did not hesitate to shoot illegally a number of animals fully listed in the weekly *Nedelya*: ten wild boars, eight roes, nineteen foxes, eight badgers, twelve mountain goats, dozens of pheasants, marmots, ducks, and so on. From the reports of the Soviet press, it was far from clear exactly where the profits from such rackets are going.

A sophisticated reader, however, well understands that the higher-ups among the country's ruling circles must reap their share. This does not mean that the middlemen—the wheelers and dealers in the shady deals and those who fence or market the merchandise—receive nothing. Furs, blue Mercedes (at least that is what *Izvestiya* says), and antique porcelain are from time to time commandeered by the party bodies from storekeepers, heads of shops, or sales personnel in order to further pad caches already rich in jewels and gold.[22]

The geography of crime in the USSR encompasses all republics, provinces, and cities, and its ethnography encompasses all peoples and nationalities. But it would be fallacious to attribute Soviet criminality to national characteristics of the Soviet people in general or of any specific Soviet nationality in particular. In the USSR, as in any contemporary society, there exists a specific pattern of criminal personality, but this pattern is not attributable to any biological, anatomical, physical, or anthropological causes. The roots of this pattern are social: it is structured by the totality of social relations.

Yet it is precisely the fact of the social origins of Soviet criminality which remains unacknowledged in the Soviet Union, as officials prefer not to recognize it or to comprehend its implications. Instead, social deviance is attributed to "objective" phenomena like demography or the quality of the labor force, or to (still!) insufficient regimentation. It is claimed that the aftereffects of World War II, which supposedly are still felt in the USSR even forty years after its termination, are responsible for the lack of manpower and indirectly are "negatively affecting a number of aspects of social life," in particular the level of conformity with legal, moral, and social conduct. The whole point is then cleverly elaborated on, the argument being that the scarcity of manpower works to the advantage of those willing to violate labor discipline and disrupt production. Recommendations stemming from such intellectual assumptions are simplicity itself: to increase the quality of labor—physical and mental labor alike—and to encourage the laborers to keep strong discipline. This is the Soviet panacea for criminality.

While the Soviet authorities are vainly attempting to introduce some order into the system of production, ever broader segments of youth and even children are being attracted to crime. The growing volume of collective and individual theft, robbery, and assaults by minors is produced by a plurality of internal motives and external factors of a varying spiritual, moral, and social nature. We refer only to the one that has been admitted by Soviet scholars, namely, the shortage of items such as stylish clothes, musical instruments, radio equipment, and certain foodstuffs.[23] Figure 1, from an analysis of data published in the Soviet Union, gives the picture of adolescent crime.

In the context of underlying social phenomena, crime in the USSR needs to be viewed as an *effect,* whereas in the context of the corrupting impact of upper-class crime on public morals it needs to be viewed as a *cause.* In the first instance, the Soviet governmental structure commands specific goals for the members of its society: the building of communism and the overcoming of the differences between mental and physical labor and between city and country. In Soviet society these goals are unrealistic, unviable, and essentially ignored. The only things valued are social status and money. Social position opens the way not only to quantitative benefits (money, privileges) but also to prestige and power. The house in which a person lives, the store in which he buys, whether he has a car and what kind—this and a great deal more depend on where a person works and what sort of position he occupies, and these are the things people seek.

Soviet social structure is not indifferent to the manner by which these aspirations are fulfilled. The official morality recommends various means for achieving these goals: study, diligence, obedience. Central among these is work. Work, it is argued, and you will achieve recognition, renown, and respect: "Work is a thing of honor, valor, and heroism." Difficulties arise when someone believing this suddenly discovers that his attainment of happiness is being obstructed by his humble origins or by his lack of the necessary connections. It is at this point—when it

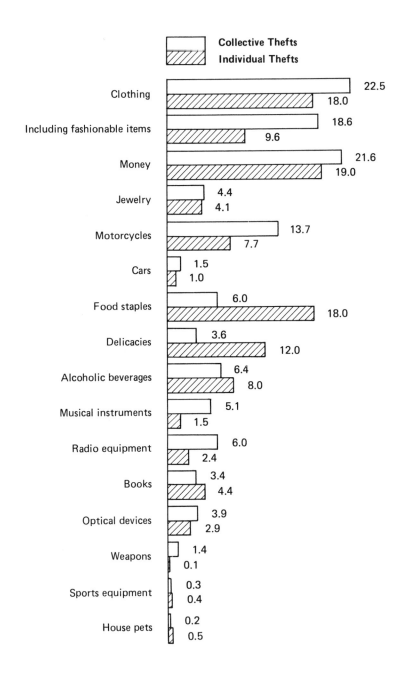

FIGURE 1. Objects Stolen by Adolescents (Individually and Collectively) as Percentages of Total Thefts

becomes apparent that the official morality effectively excludes the majority from attaining goals it has been encouraged to seek—that the legal but ineffectual means gradually give way to more effective, less legal methods. The tendency arises to evaluate means not in terms of morality or legality but only and above all in terms of their results. Deceit, corruption, and fraud become more and more common as the goal of achieving success becomes increasingly disjointed from the prescribed means. In other words, when the goal justifies the means, abstract, impractical morality disintegrates and collapses.

Soviet propaganda strives to create the impression, within the country but even more intensively abroad, that crime is the doing of only the lowest classes. This is supported by Soviet criminology and otherwise nonexistent statistics on crime. In the information for the masses, the facts are cleverly and skillfully selected to create the impression that crime in the world of the elite exists only as an incidental, isolated phenomenon. That was never the case in the past, when by means of violence and deceit the Communist class forced its way to power, nor does it reflect present Soviet reality when that class rules society by evading laws and trampling morality for the sake of its goals. These goals are always a career, and sometimes enrichment as well. In the race for power and self-affirmation, the Communists constantly and willingly cross the boundary of the law, assuming not without foundation that the likely gain will compensate with interest for any unlikely unpleasant consequences. Not only waste and theft, but also deception to cover up abuses already perpetrated and those being prepared, has reached epidemic proportions in elite circles. Swindle, graft, bribery, misinformation—these are the stepping-stones to power, the road to well-being and a secure, prestigious existence. Everything that surrounds the Soviet man in his daily life—his apartment, furniture, clothing, the food he eats, everything he uses throughout his life, up to and including the coffin in which he is buried—if not produced by breaking the law, is certainly sold in defiance of it.

Under the monopolistic governmental system of communism, crime becomes the real content of domestic policy, and domestic policy becomes the basis for crime. In some instances political power is the prerequisite for economic corruption, and in other instances corruption is the means of acquiring power. When it is possible to calculate the damage done by crimes committed by Communists, that damage will undoubtedly be seen to have been greater than that resulting from burglaries, robberies, and other acts performed by professional criminals. At present, however, this damage cannot be fully and precisely assessed, if only because criminals from elite circles are as a rule not exposed and are not brought to trial. Is it surprising that under these circumstances the social prestige of honest labor in the USSR is falling, that plundering, stealing, and filching from the government is considered good business?

This system of social values has a pernicious effect on the ethical basis of Soviet law and order. It leads the Soviet citizen to commit crimes. As a matter of fact, people who embark on the path of professional crime quickly come to the conclusion that the methods by which they enrich themselves differ in no way from those by which Soviet political figures achieve success. Moreover, by raising their social status, the Soviet citizens gain a useful shield against legal prosecution.

Notes

1. M. Onufriev, *Russiya v reformakh* (Russia in Reforms) (St. Petersburg, 1914), p. 81.

2. In the collection *Trud i chelovek* (Labor and Man), *vyp. 2: Informatsionny byulleten' AN SSSR i Sovetskoy Sotsiologicheskoy Assotsiatsii,* No. 73 (izd. Instituta konkretnykh sotsial'nykh issledovanii, Moscow, 1972), pp. 77–78, we read:

> For the first time in our country, sociologists had the opportunity to acquaint themselves with the materials of the Central Statistical Board [i.e., with secret materials] and were able to calculate the expenditures of the population of the country as a whole and individually, according to different social groups, on the basis of the balance of financial revenues.
>
> The social balance of financial revenues and expenditures of the population testifies to a certain disproportion in the distribution of incomes of the population. In particular, more than a third—35.8 percent—of the aggregated wage fund is distributed among 10 percent of the workers: officials of the party-government appartus, military cadres, industrial and agricultural workers, and research workers. These data indicate that, under socialist conditions, there are still serious disproportions in the incomes of the population. Every year the prosperity of the population increases. Nonetheless, it

is evident that there is still some disproportion in the distribution of the incomes of the population, as calculated on per capita equivalent. In general in the country, the income in families of party officials averages 157–161 rubles, of military personnel—146 rubles, and of researchers—131 rubles. These findings, of course, must not be considered conclusive, since the study on this problem has not been completed. . . .

Over ten years have passed since *Labor and Man* was published. New material from Soviet sociological studies, which I succeeded in becoming acquainted with at the International Sociological Congress in Mexico in 1982, did not reveal considerable change in the system of income distribution in the Soviet Union. I consider it feasible to cite these studies since they are more current, although it is very difficult to evaluate their accuracy.

3. "Partiynaya rabota i partiiny rabotnik" (Party Work and Party Official), in *Ideologicheskaya rabota* (Ideological Work), Izd. AON TsK KPSS (Moscow, 1972), pp. 138–139, 144; M. Voslensky, *Nomenclatura* (London: Overseas Publications Interchange, 1984), pp. 322–323; Ilya Zemtsov, "Ideology," *Lexicon of Soviet Political Terms* (Fairfax, Va.: Hero Books, 1984).

4. *Trud i chelovek,* p. 132.

5. Ibid., p. 124.

6. "The elderly mother of my acquaintance, an honored collective farm worker who can no longer work, receives a pension of 5 rubles a month. One of my acquaintances, a highly educated woman and an art historian, receives 25 rubles a month (and has no other means of support). An enormous number of people do not receive any pension, since they do not fall within the boundaries of the law (a document is required officially stating the length of service in a government enterprise). . . . However, if you have special (political) merit, your pension can reach 200 rubles or over a month" (A. Fedoseev, *Zapadnya* [The Trap] [Frankfurt am Main: Possev Verlag, 1976], p. 300).

7. According to other sources, the official average wage is 120 rubles a month (see ibid., p. 297).

8. A. Sergeev, *Sotsializm i trud* (Socialism and Labor) (Moscow: Nauka, 1976), pp. 84–85. See also Lev Losev, *Zhratva* (Gorging) (Ann Arbor: Hermitage Publishers, 1984), pp. 77, 79, 82.

9. The author arrived at these data on the basis of an analysis of the increase in the gross national products of the USSR and the United States, as cited in the Western and Soviet press in 1976, 1982, and 1983.

10. See the report of the Central Committee of the Communist Party of the Soviet Union, "Ocherednye zadachi partii v oblasti vnutrennei i vneshnei politiki" (The Next Tasks of the Party in the Areas of Domes-

tic and Foreign Policy), Congress of the Communist Party of the Soviet Union, stenog. record (Moscow, 1976), pp. 87–115, speech of the General Secretary of the Central Committee of the CPSU Comrade Yu. V. Andropov at the Plenum of the Central Committee of the CPSU on June 15, 1983, *Pravda*, June 16, 1983.

11. See A. Cherednichenko, "Tvoe zdorov'e, Kolya" (Your Health, Kolja), *Komsomol'skaya pravda*, May 17, 1978; R. Lirman, "Protiv estetizatsii p'yanstva" (Against Romanticizing Drunkenness), *Sovetskaya kul'tura*, June 30, 1978; V. V. Kudryavtsev, "The Research Problem of Social Deviance," *Sotsiologicheskie issledovaniya* 2 (1983): 113.

12. "Ann and I were having dinner with a young biologist and we marveled at the good, freshly butchered beef that his wife had served. It was far better than the meat I had seen in state stores. But he said he had bought it in an ordinary state store, for 3.20 rubles a kilo ($1.92 a pound), about 60 percent over the fixed price" (Hedrick Smith, *The Russians* [London: Sphere Books, 1976], p. 100; Losev, *Zhratva*, pp. 52–64).

13. "A workman told me he had paid 50 rubles ($66) to the surgeon in a state hospital for operating on his legs after he fell down an elevator shaft, and a chauffeur said he paid 150 rubles to have three of his wife's teeth capped" (Smith, *The Russians*, p. 113).

14. "Iz zala suda" (From the Courtroom), *Bakinsky rabochy*, August 9, 1978; "Nakazan za zloupotreblenie" (Punished for Abuse of Office), *Pravda*, July 11, 1984.

15. A. Gladilin, "Krasnodarskaya mafiya" (The Krasnodar Mafia), *Novoe russkoe slovo*, October 1, 1978.

16. Ilya Zemtsov, *Partiya ili Mafiya* (Party or Mafia) (Paris: YMCA Press, 1976); "Report of G. A. Aliev at the Plenum of the Central Committee of the Communist Party of Azerbaijan on October 22, 1982," *Vyshka*, October 24, 1982.

17. Ilya Zemtsov, *Struggle for Power in the Kremlin, I: Andropov* (Fairfax, Va.: Hero Books, 1984); A. Yashvili, "Razgrom podpol'nogo biznesa" (The Destruction of Underground Business). *Posev* (1973): 32–33.

18. "Prokuror-vymogatel' " (The Prosecutor-Blackmailer), *Bakinsky rabochy*, July 30, 1978; "Vserëz o raznom" (Seriously About Various Matters), *Izvestiya*, July 11, 1984.

19. Yashvili, "Razgrom podpol'nogo biznesa," p. 32.

20. "Prokuror-vymogatel'."

21. "Iz zala suda—rasplata" (From the Courtroom—Retribution),

Bakinsky rabochy, July 15, 1978; A. Vaksberg, "Vse bilety prodany" (All the Tickets Have Been Sold), *Literaturnaya gazeta,* October 18, 1978; "Iz zala suda—raskhititeley zerna—k otvetu" (From the Courtroom—Plunderers of Grain—Toward an Answer), *Bakinsky rabochy,* August 13, 1978.

22. "Ukreplyat' partiynuyu i gosudarstvennuyu distsiplinu, uluchshat' nadzor i vospitanie kadrov" (To Strengthen Party and Government Discipline, to Improve Supervision and Education of Cadres), *Partiinaya zhizn'* 14 (July 1984), p. 19; "Professor s karabinom" (Professor with a Rifle), *Nedelya* 33 (1984); "Sladkaya zhizn'" (*La Dolce Vita*), *Izvestiya,* November 16, 1984.

23. V. A. Kudryavtsev, "Issledovatel'skaya problema-sotsial'nye otkloneniya" (The Research Problem of Social Deviance), *Sotsiologicheskie issledovaniya* 2 (1983):114–115; V. I. Litvinov, "Motivatsionnaya struktura gruppovykh pravonarusheniy nesovershennoletnikh" (The Motivational Structure of Group Law-Breaking by Minors), *Sotsiologicheskie issledovaniya* 2 (1983): 132–135.

Chapter 2

Nonmercenary Plutocrats

Every Leninist knows, if he is a true Leninist, that equalization in the
consumer field is simply reactionary petty-bourgeois stupidity.
—Stalin, *Voprosy Leninizma* (Issues of Leninism), Moscow

Money is the true and absolute lubricant for the lopsided, falter-
ing Soviet social-political machine. In the USSR, money is essential for attaining a high position, for remaining in it, for
extending it. Thus, if accumulation and profiteering are not the
only passions of the nomenclatura functionary, he at any rate
indulges in them with great fervor. This should come as no sur-
prise to the founders of the Soviet state. The inconsistency between limitless power and limited compensation was the reason
that the Communist ruling class constantly felt a need for sums
far exceeding compensation received. And so it inevitably developed and displayed great ingenuity in meeting that need.

Aside from their basic salaries, in the elite circles of Soviet
society—executives of the Central Committee of the party, the
government, the Komsomol, the trade unions, the Supreme
Soviet, the generals, the attorney general's office, the Academy
of Sciences, the editorial boards of the central newspapers, and
so on—thousands and possibly tens of thousands of functionaries ruling the USSR receive special subsidies to their
salaries, called "Kremlin rations." This custom originated in the
1920s, when the bankruptcy of the Leninist policy of equalizing,
by which the salary of a party functionary did not exceed the pay
of a skilled worker, became apparent. For years the communists
could not deviate from this principle of compensation: in a workers' government, based on the dictatorship of the proletariat, no
one had the right to earn more than the source of his authority,
the workers (an exception was made only for foreigners and

bourgeois specialists, who were considered foreigners). But in the 1920s this tradition became increasingly more difficult to uphold: the most qualified specialists were leaving the party, the government apparatus, and the management of the national economy for private industry. A solution had to be found, and preferably one that did not require abandoning the above-mentioned sacred principle. The issuance of Kremlin rations as a supplement to the salaries of executives was such a solution. During the years of economic depression and hunger in the USSR, the ration was paid in kind, but beginning with the 1930s it was paid in money: 32 rubles for nomenclatura officials on the Union level, 18 rubles for leading officials on the provincial or city level. But these were not ordinary Soviet rubles, which at that time were not worth much because of the unstable exchange rate. The money was linked to the official price of gold (1 gram of gold = 1 ruble). The years passed. The USSR had long since retreated from the equalization principle. The salary of a top government official, outstanding scientist, or high-ranking military officer came to exceed the average salary of a worker by five or six times. But the custom was preserved: the Soviet elite, in addition to their salaries, receive Kremlin rations, which according to tradition are linked to the rate of exchange of the ruble of the 1920s (1 ruble = 1 gram of gold). What this means when translated into ordinary ruble prices becomes obvious when the purchasing power of the ordinary ruble and the gold ruble of the Kremlin ration are compared.

Table 3 shows that the purchasing power of the Kremlin ration ruble is eight to ten times higher than that of the ordinary ruble. Therefore, the basic salary of a Soviet executive is fattened by 160–300 rubles, depending on the category of the ration to which he is entitled.[1] Equally important, he purchases all he needs not through the ordinary commercial network, with its severely limited selection of goods, but in special stores where he can buy high-quality products at fixed prices and in any quantity. The network of these stores extends throughout the entire country, reaching into every republic, every district, and every Soviet city. Their purpose is to protect the Soviet elite from the chronic

Table 3
Retail Prices in Government and Cooperative Trade Shops in
Ordinary Rubles and in Gold-Equivalent Kremlin Ration Rubles

		Price in Ordinary Rubles*	Price in Gold Rubles†
White bread	kg.	0.23	0.05
Beef	kg.	2.00	0.30
Sausages	kg.	2.20	0.25
Potatoes	kg.	0.10	0.03
Sugar	kg.	0.90	0.20
Butter	kg.	3.60	0.40
Margarine	kg.	1.80	0.20
Cooking oil	liter	1.70	0.15
Milk	liter	0.30	0.04
Eggs	10	0.90	0.10
Vodka	liter	8.24	1.50
Cigarettes	20	0.32	0.40

*See "Radio Liberty Research," May 6, 1978.

†Extracted from "Prilozheniya k spravochniku Upravdelami TsK KPSS" (Appendix to the Guide to the Administrative Departments of the Central Committee of the Communist Party of the Soviet Union) (Moscow, 1977), pp. 17–18.

shortages and irregularities of supply, furnishing the privileged classes with delicacies.

The Soviet system of stores for the ruling elite has its strict protocol. There are special "closed" stores, which sell at reduced prices, intended for high Soviet figures who are not entitled to Kremlin rations but whose high social status makes it unseemly for them to shop in ordinary stores. Here the assortment of items is broad, not as extensive as that in the stores for holders of Kremlin rations but unfailingly offering their customers first-rate merchandise. There are also distribution centers for the most favored—members of the Central Committee and ministers—which supply their homes with hot dishes prepared by Kremlin chefs. All such places are located away from busy streets, in unpretentious quarters, so as not to attract the attention and envy of the toiling masses.

Certain circles of Soviet society, while not part of the elite, are intermediate between the ruling and the middle classes. Those in this category are people whose status has not yet been definitely determined. Some will rise and in time enter the ruling class; some, more numerous, will recede back into the middle class after a certain period in this transitional state. These are deputies of various Soviets and members of various plenums—party, trade union, and Komsomol members who owe their positions to the need to maintain the decorum of Soviet democracy, which demands a certain representation of workers, peasants, and intelligentsia in the elected organs of the party and the executive committees of the Soviets.

The impermanence of the status of the people in this intermediate category is reflected in the unstable nature of their privileges. They are not permitted to use the private government and semi-government stores on a permanent basis, except during the plenary sessions of the organizations they represent. Thus, for the session of the Supreme Soviet or the plenary sessions of the provincial, town, or regional party committees, the delegates receive, along with their mandates, one-time coupons allowing them to shop in the government distribution centers. These coupons serve as a hint of possible future bliss, if the appropriate loyalty is manifested—and if not, if one does not demonstrate appropriate obedience and diligence, there is the prospect of the privileges being taken away. This indeed is something to fear, for privileges in the USSR, the dividends paid on social position, are more valuable than money. They are the testimony to prestige.

For the faithful, for those who serve the privileged class with proper devotion and who themselves belong to its lower echelons, there exists in the Soviet Union a chain of stores known as "Berëzka." In these stores goods are sold not for devalued Soviet rubles but for certificates that Soviet citizens working abroad or attached to institutions with foreign connections receive as part of their salary (work abroad is a status symbol in the USSR). In these stores the citizen with certificates (special coupons) can buy at reasonable prices foreign goods that are in short supply in the USSR.

As for those who have been mobilized to build communism—

the ordinary citizens—they are forced to wander through stores for long hours after work in search, in one store, of no-longer-fresh frozen meat, in another, of salami, in a third, of eggs. The lot of the toiling masses is exhausting, hours-long queuing. Here is an account by a writer who emigrated from the USSR and settled in Israel, which was subsequently published in the Israeli press:

> In the town of V. there is neither meat nor salami. . . . For the town's inhabitants, about once a week and sometimes less often, smoked bones, the waste products of the local meat plant complex, are brought to hurriedly set-up street stalls or to the open market for sale to the population. . . .
>
> They sell them in bulk, a whole carcass at a time, each one weighing 15–20 kg. The goods are delivered unwrapped. A great power cannot manage to solve a paper shortage. Heaving it onto their shoulders or thrusting it into large bast sacks, the inhabitants of the town of V. drag home the bones for which they waited so long in line. They carry them hurriedly across the gaily decorated, festive-looking streets. And on their faces are inspiration and joy—there were enough bones for them to get some. And behind them at the stalls there is the noise of the worried people in line—will there be enough for the rest?!
>
> Music is playing. On the roof along the facade of the big grocery store on the same block, in which there has been no meat or salami for weeks, in which salesgirls in white aprons yawn from boredom, in meter-high letters embossed on red calico flapping in the wind, are written the words of the great dictator: "Our chief goal is *concern for the well-being of the people.*"

Gloomy, sad, sorrowful queues, like ghosts, follow Soviet citizens everywhere all through their lives. This peculiarity of Soviet life has found its way even into the vocabulary of the Russian language. They don't say "to buy" *(kupit')*, but rather "to acquire" *(dostat')* (i.e., under the counter).

The lines are for everyone, save for the ruling class.[2] Places are reserved for the elite at premieres in theaters and in movie theaters, and in any hotel, restaurant, railway station, or airport a certain number of places are reserved for their needs, or if not for real needs then "just in case." This is stipulated in the regulations. If the places are not used for whatever reason, they are put on sale at the very last moment. It matters little, however, if they are or are not sold. This loss is taken into consideration beforehand.[3]

The ruling class in the USSR has won for itself other special privileges as well. Its life passes in a different dimension from that of the people. Communism has institutionalized one standard of living for the masses and another for those with power. As part of its "dolce vita" the ruling class has created palatial hospitals—spacious, beautifully furnished, located in pine forests or on the seashore, so perfect that a Soviet writer recuperating in one of them remarked, "Here is communism in eighty beds!"[4] A totally different sort of medicine is practiced in these hospitals, where everything, even the research, is secret. Since the people have no possibility of receiving such treatment, it is best that they do not know about it. Other levels of prestigious hospitals are those of the KGB, the ministry of internal affairs, the ministry of defense, and the Academy of Sciences—all somewhat less luxurious but still very different from the wretched clinics for the people.

The ruling class benefits not only from special hospitals but also from sanatoriums and resorts offering a wide variety of climates. For the ruling class, separate compartments on planes, special coaches on trains, special waiting rooms in railway stations and airports, and so on, are reserved. To keep the elite separated from the simple people, they are given season tickets to concerts and theaters as well as passes that allow them to obtain tickets out of turn. Not only do they have personal cars while on vacations or business trips, they also receive coupons for free taxi rides.

In the Soviet Union it is not the usual but rather a communist arithmetic that operates, according to which one-third of the national income is distributed among the privileged 10 percent. The remainder, after those who are closer to authority seize the best and the most, goes to the people, the toilers of communism, in full accordance with their "rights." The naive, those unable to understand the principles of proletarian equality, are told that this is the logic of class democracy. Under the conditions of such class-defined morality, the Soviet political leader had to become corrupt, and he did.

Initially, it appeared that the increases in salaries and privileges—and not a year of Soviet power went by without their increasing—would prevent corruption among the representatives of the ruling class, but they only whetted the appetite for more. The ruling class continued to view the government as a source of wealth, the main thing being to line one's pockets as fully as possible. It would be a mistake, therefore, to view their criminal machinations as incidental, isolated, or exceptional in Soviet social life. Instead, they form a fantastic webbing from which the fabric of Soviet life is woven, a pattern in which stealing is not a private affair but rather depends on a well-organized system of fraudulence that extends through and beyond the government-party-economic apparatus. For the high Soviet official, therefore, salary is not the essential thing. He does welcome a five-digit salary, but the determining factor for him is still his career.

In the USSR a career gives a person what cannot be acquired with money—power over the fate of people, recognition, honor. Yet the top bureaucrats do squeeze a great many material benefits from their positions. In the Soviet Union each rung of the social hierarchy has its specific advantages: a larger apartment, a better supply of consumer goods, a personal car, a trip abroad. (To isolate the Soviet social structure from the influence of other systems, the ruling class maintains international contacts only through its highly trusted figures, and even then extremely selectively.) The essence of this good fortune cannot be understood unless one grasps that wealth and poverty in the Soviet Union are measured by the quantity of things in one's personal position. Even if one has the means, these cannot always be bought. Something is always in short supply, something has always temporarily disappeared from the market.

Nevertheless, salary has a significance for the Communist ruling class that is by no means symbolic. People save money, hide it in cellars, convert it into gold and valuables, and in general regard it in such a way that anyone who gets near another's stash takes his life into his hands. Thus, while salary is perhaps not the main thing in life for the Communist ruling class, those "non-mercenary plutocrats," it is certainly not a trifling matter.

What motivates the Soviet citizen? For many, it is evidently the desire to live, to enjoy life, to love, and to be loved. But once these primary needs of the Soviet elite are met, the main motivation becomes a persistent, stubborn, overriding need to get as much lucre as possible, by any and every means.

Having observed the representatives of the ruling class for many years, the author feels qualified to state that a move from one department to another is usually dictated only by greed and self-interest. The determining motive is not ambition or a desire for independent work, but rather a desire for both the aboveboard and the under-the-table opportunities and privileges inherent in the new assignment. One has only to promise a Soviet partocrat 1,000 rubles more and he will leave any work, a secure position, a lovingly furnished apartment, his familiar circle of friends, and rush off to any out-of-the-way place—to the tundra, the Arctic Circle, the bare desert. The newspapers do not fail to praise this hero for his selflessness and readiness to be where he is needed, but I would say to be where he himself needs to be.

A party career may not be the only way, but it is certainly the surest way to amass a fortune in the USSR. It opens up an extremely wide range of opportunities. By remaining in the bosom of party work, a person is guaranteed not only a high salary and many rights and privileges but also a monthly income in the form of bribes and gifts from the departments and organizations he is charged with supervising. The amount of his compensation is directly proportional to his status.

After a period of time it is sometimes possible to transfer into industry or government. When making such a move, the exchange value of the party worker is considerable: an official of the Central Committee is regarded at least as equal to an assistant minister on the republic level or to the head of an important national managerial board *(Glavk)*. Although such a move does have its advantages—by nearing the source of underground capital, the former party functionary can now quickly enrich himself—a price must be paid. Not only does he step out of the superprivileged partocratic caste, but the former party worker now must work harder, has broader responsibility, and is thus answerable for more. However, there is hope that he will not be forgotten—if he conducts himself with a degree of decorum, maintains his contacts with the party apparatus, and remembers to divide his profits (preferably in cash, but valuable presents and expensive dinners will also do). If he does all this, his old buddies may again draw him into the party apparatus at some new political conjuncture—naturally, into some prestigious position.

For an official of the Central Committee of the Communist Party it is highly desirable to move on to independent party work, on the province level. This arouses considerable respect: it means that a man's time has come. The position of a secretary of a provincial committee awaits him, although not that of first secretary, which is for those a bit higher in rank. Yet if he demonstrates a certain resoluteness by maintaining current contacts and cultivating new ones, there is a distinct possibility that he may return to the central party apparatus, perhaps as head of a sector of the Central Committee. After some more time has passed, he can return to the province from which he emerged, this time as one familiar with local conditions, in the capacity of secretary of the provincial committee.

A first secretary is the elite of the elite. He is given candidate membership in the Central Committee, deputation in the Supreme Soviet, and direct contact with the General Secretary. From there on, the main thing is not to slip. If a first secretary of a provincial committee (or city committee) knows how to submit his work for approval and knows how to impress the Politburo with his seriousness of purpose, his sociability, and his sense of obligation, if he fulfills his duty and unobtrusively learns to foresee and anticipate the wishes of his superiors, he will be rewarded. From the rank of "feudal prince," the governor-general of a province, he will make his way into the court itself and become a secretary of the Central Committee of the CPSU. Once there, if he stays clear of risky intrigues, he will rise further—to the Politburo, where he will be honored as leader, his portrait raised high to accolades, applause, and stormy ovations.

The picture we have drawn is a generalization, abstracted from a great many cases, including cases of stumbling along the way. There are many ambitious party bureaucrats who, not knowing how to be of service to their boss or because of unfavorable political circumstances, were ejected from the party center as an example to others. Thrust out to the caprices of fate, they were doomed to end their days in some out-of-the-way province, region, or city as third or even fourth secretary. One should not, however, pity such failures; a fine dacha (country cottage), a personal pension, and a fat bank account await them in their old age.

Central Committee officials who are a bit more clever do not want to tempt fate. Having learned from the mistakes of their colleagues, and being perhaps a bit more intelligent than the rest, they decide to get off the party merry-go-round in time. They prepare for this step slowly and carefully, by providing themselves with Candidate's and then Doctor's degrees. There are always highly educated toadies and bootlickers around who are ready to write dissertations for them. When opportunity knocks, the Central Committee official suddenly emerges as director of a scientific research institute, and then, after a time, succeeds in pushing his way into the Academy of Sciences, first as a corresponding member then, with some luck, as a full member.

It is debatable which is more profitable: membership in the Central Committee or membership in the Academy. But one thing is certain: to be an academician is more peaceful and more stable. The salaries are lower and the possibilities for graft are much less, but opportunities are not lacking. There are always the fees for graduate students, while coauthorship of books others write also carries a sizable fee. The title "academician" guarantees a person the chairmanship of a department at a university which pays 500 rubles a month, and another 500 a month is received for membership in the Academy. To this should be added the Kremlin rations, a personal car, and a government dacha. Membership on the numerous scientific councils, editorial boards, and commissions is also worth a great deal in terms of money and prestige. In addition, there is always the possibility that the respected academician who grew up on party work will someday be summoned to the Central Committee. In this case the least that awaits him is management of a department and perhaps even a secretaryship. This is the way the cards of power are played, and many Soviet academicians have passed through the stages of this game: Pospelov, Mitin, and Konstantinov. As for Ponomarev, Egorov, Afanasev, Arbatov, and Gvishiani, they are still in the midst of play.

The opportunities of a party career are limitless, even for someone who does not have the luck to begin with the Central Committee. The regional party committee is not a bad start either. In the space of two or three years it is possible to switch over from being an official of the regional committee to head of the regional police department, regional attorney general, director of a plant, or head of the regional department of people's education. While these are not very exalted positions, they are lucrative. Having passed through the first corridors of power— the regional committee, the city committee, and the provincial committee (the amount of time and effort required is usually proportional to the origins and connections of the person)—the beginning party worker, if he has self-control and patience, is sure to reach the Central Committee of the CPSU. Further progress beyond this level of success has already been described.

Party functionaries are the watchdogs of the regime, and in this capacity they are well paid for their services. Their salaries compete only with those of well-known figures in the arts and sports, and perhaps with the scientific and military elite. Table 4 shows how great a gap there is between the earnings of highly skilled workers and senior party figures.

The monthly salaries of first secretaries of party committees are as follows. First secretaries of regional committees receive 580 rubles per month; those of city committees (with a population of more than 100,000) receive 700 rubles; those of provincial committees receive 800; and those of territorial committees and the Central Committees of the republics receive 900 rubles a month. In addition, first secretaries receive certain supplements (plus numerous free social services and other privileges). As a rule, first secretaries of the regional committees are deputies of the Supreme Soviet of the autonomous and Union republics;

Table 4

Monthly Incomes (in Rubles) for 1977 of a Senior Party Functionary and a Highly Skilled Worker

Nature of Employment	Salary	Kremlin Ration*	Increment for Deputation in the Supreme Soviet	Monthly Money Value of Family Vacation Pass to Sanatorium†	Monthly Money Value of Medical Allowance	Total
First secretary, regional committee	580	160	50	50–60	49	889–899
First secretary, city committee	700	300	100	80–100	59	1,239–1,259
First secretary, provincial committee	800	300	100	80–100	66	1,346–1,366
First secretary, territorial committee or Central Committee of a republic	900	300	100	80–100	75	1,455–1,475
Highly skilled worker	160	—	—	6–7‡	—	166–167

Source: Salaries of party officials are based on data cited in the collection *Ideologicheskaya rabota* (Ideological Work) (Moscow: Publishing House of the Academy of Social Sciences, 1967), in the article "Partiinaya rabota i partiinyi rabotnik" (Party Work and the Party Official), pp. 123–126, as supplemented and detailed by data reported by I. M. Popova and V. G. Moin, "Zarplata kak sotsial'naya tsennost'" (Salary as a Social Indicator of Value), *Sotsiologicheskie issledovaniya* 2 (1983): 109–110; by O. M. Novikov, "Raspredelenie po trudu—khozraschet i tsenoobrazovanie" (Distribution According to Labor—Economic Calculation and Price-Formation), *Sotsiologicheskie issledovaniya* 3 (1983): 92–99; and by M. N. Rutkevich, "Sotsialistichesky obraz zhizni: kachestvennaya i kolichestvennaya opredelennost'" (The Socialist Way of Life: Qualitative and Quantitative Definition), in ibid., 3, pp. 9–16.

Note: Data here is reported for 1977. Because in the following eight years there has not been a marked change in the *official* salary of top party functionaries, the figures reflect the current (1985) situation as well.

*The Kremlin ration is calculated in terms of real purchasing power.

†Passes to sanatoriums and resorts include the price for all members of the family, assuming a family of three to four persons.

‡The cost of a pass to a trade union resort is 72 rubles. Under the best of circumstances, a worker will receive such a pass once in ten years.

deputation means another 50 rubles added to the salary. Once a year they receive a free pass to a government sanatorium, the nominal cost of which amounts to from 240 to 320 rubles, and once a year they receive a thirteenth salary, the so-called medical allowance. The supplements to the salaries of first secretaries of city, provincial, territorial and Central Committees are even greater. The free passes they receive are also for members of their families (a party worker on the regional level must pay 25 percent of the cost of the pass for his wife and 50 percent for his children). City, provincial, and republic secretaries also act as deputies to the Supreme Soviet, which adds another 100 rubles per month. The medical allowance is also higher in proportion to the salary.

An exact reckoning would also take into account the entire spectrum of services, privileges, and rights enjoyed by first secretaries and would add another 30 to 40 percent to their incomes. Deputies to the Supreme Soviet enjoy free use of all forms of public transportation; for deputies of the republics, within the borders of the republic, and for national deputies, throughout the country. They are also given personal cars and a staff of chauffeurs. Moreover, a sizable portion of expense money partocrats get for official receptions, business trips, inspection tours, and so forth, winds up in the partocrat's own pocket. But even discounting all these supplementary benefits, the income of a highly placed party functionary is still six to nine times greater than that of a highly skilled worker. The Soviet worker is not able to take free trips, and only one worker out of many thousand is selected to be a deputy; even then, as a rule, he is a deputy to a local soviet, for which he is not paid. As for the right to a free rest home stay, at best this is available once in ten years. Nevertheless, we have added an additional 6 rubles to his monthly salary (which amounts to 72 rubles annually) since this is what a pass to a trade union rest home costs.

What is behind such generous compensation for party bureaucrats? They are certainly not being paid for their executive ability, initiative, or creativity. Given his instinct for self-preservation, the party functionary consistently avoids any significant decisions—anything that might affect accepted canons. True, by the nature of the social role they play, party bureaucrats participate in the development of government decisions and have a measure of responsibility for various public actions, but their recommendations could be made just as well, if not better, by a computer. The true function of their high salary is to insulate them from doubts about the work they perform and to isolate them from the people. As long as this buffer zone is strong and viable, the ruling elite has no reason to worry. Vague dissatisfaction and grumblings filtering up from the masses will not disturb their tranquillity and well-being. And any order or directive filtering down from above, no matter how absurd or senseless, will invariably find an executor and a victim.

The partocrat can be linked to the cormorant, the wild sea bird used in fishing in Japan. Around the bird's neck is tied a string that allows it to breathe but prevents it from swallowing fish; the bird thus obediently brings fish to the master's boat. At feeding times, the string around its neck is loosened, and then it can catch one or two fish for itself. The party functionary is also permitted to fish for himself, even to be in the pay of clever underground businessmen. The latter is often necessary if he is to bring in a catch for his masters. Although the precise thickness to which he in this way lines his pockets is difficult to determine, something can be said about the nature and magnitude of this additional income.

The secretary of the party committee of an industrial region accumulates sums that far exceed his formal salary. This illicit income is derived from obligatory tributes and dues from various enterprises and from sums given by administrative organs—the police, judges, prosecutors. The secretary of the party committee of a rural region accumulates about as much, the loss of industrial income being compensated for by payments from collective and state farms. Naturally the nature of the enterprise and the financial condition of the cooperative enterprises are significant factors.

The total incomes of regional secretaries are a function of various factors, among them the region's geography, traditions, and the national composition of its inhabitants. The take of the regional party leadership in capital cities is somewhat smaller:

the powerful network of city, provincial, and republic bosses hangs over him, demanding and exacting their share. Also relevant is whether there is a university or other institution of higher learning in the region. The presence of such an institution increases the amount of tribute. If the region has hotels, restaurants, and places of entertainment, a monthly tribute is exacted from each of these. Also swelling the secretary's takings are certain one-time but very profitable operations. At least once a month either a periodic reorganization is planned and new salaried vacancies are opened up, or the apartments in a new building are to be distributed, or applicants are being accepted into a university or an institute. No event takes place without the sanction of the regional committee, and approval of the party leadership in the USSR costs a great deal of money. Even after the required sums are paid to the high-ranking party bosses, the regional secretary is still guaranteed a monthly income that is incomparably higher than his salary.

We are talking about substantial sums indeed. An indication of how substantial is provided by the going price of the job of first secretary of a regional committee. It is an unwritten rule in the USSR that the price of an important job should not exceed a year's income yielded by it. The position should return the capital invested and yield a good profit within a few years, since the fate of a party worker makes it impossible to plan on more than one four-year term. As for the price of the position of first secretary of a regional committee, it is always many tens of thousands, and in southern and eastern Soviet republics it is easily hundreds of thousands.

Indirect facts from records of Soviet criminal proceedings of the 1970s and 1980s also support our contentions. The head of the Tbilisi Medical Institute, holder of many ranks and titles (member of the Central Committee of the Georgian Communist Party, Deputy of the Supreme Soviet, Honored Scientist, Professor, Doctor, etc.), demanded and received 40,000 rubles from candidates for admission to the medical institute. It was, of course, possible not to pay, but without the bribe, admission to the institute was impossible. When the director's crime was uncovered, he was found to have 15 million rubles in cash. He had worked seven years—net profit per year: 2,150,000 rubles. Not much imagination is needed to project what sort of income the secretary of the regional party committee that administered the medical institute must have had, considering that all hiring and enrollment at the institute was sanctioned and controlled by the representatives of the regional committee.

There is a specific geography of graft in the Soviet Union. In Georgia, Azerbaijan, and Armenia, according to tradition, a great many bribes are given and taken, such behavior being considered almost lawful. There is less black capital in Russia proper than in the Transcaucasian republics. Although the medical institutes in the former areas are headed by scientists of no less renown than those to whom medical education is entrusted in Georgia (the director of the Moscow Stomatology Institute, A. Belousov, was assistant minister of health of the USSR and head of the Medical Department of the Central Committee), bribes there are somewhat less—in Moscow, 15,000–20,000 rubles. In Kalinin, a city northwest of Moscow, and in Riga, west of Moscow, admission to a medical institute costs 5,000 rubles. Far to the east, however, as well as to the south, in the city of Tashkent the bribes for admission to the medical institute are the highest in the USSR.[5] One cannot, of course, estimate the incomes of party secretaries directly on the basis of the kickbacks these party functionaries receive from medical colleges or from other kinds of illegal deals, but there is undoubtedly a correlation between profits from under-the-table deals and the incomes of regional party secretaries.

In the geography of bribes in the USSR, there are no blank spaces. No party leader is above taking them. In the depths of Russia, in poor places with an impoverished population, like Omsk or Tambov, it would seem that there would not be anything for the secretary to take. The result is that in such places the party rulers limit themselves to taking payment in kind: while inspecting the hunting grounds, they take salmon and black caviar; from the collective and state farms they invariably return with a leg of beef or pork; and from the factories they get traditional bottles of cognac.

What we are speaking of, then, is a general abuse of power in the USSR, corruption based on the very nature of the communist regime in which government is the privilege of only one class—the nomenclatura. Material well-being in this society is strictly proportional to the rung in the hierarchy on which a person is located, which determines not only the amount but also the source of his income, and not only the opportunity for acquiring these benefits but also the possibilities for distributing them. Still, it is not our intention to suggest that party functionaries are the only perpetrators of crime in the Soviet Union, the only ones with a lust for acquisition. Respected managers of industry and agriculture, those directly responsible for creating black capital, have appetites no less expansive or expensive. They feed all the links in the governmental and social apparatus and amass substantial fortunes, but they have less than the party elite, and they risk more.

The basic technique of underground business is quite simple and relies on manipulation of raw materials not included in the plan and on inflated prices. The scale of black capital, however, would be the envy of some Western practitioners. Underground business encompasses the food industry, household products, the chemical industry, and consumer items. The selling methods vary. Goods are sold for cash through stores or on an order basis through offices and organizations. Records and accounts are kept in two sets of books, one for "legal" and one for "illegal" production. When illicit production exceeds half the total production of the enterprise and keeping parallel records becomes too complicated, fictitious enterprises are created. Such enterprises, existing only on paper, have their own address, staff, employees, plan, and inevitably their own bank account. The underground goods are attributed on paper in this way to a legal producer in whose name a contract is drawn up and to whom the capital investment is transferred. Work plans are drawn up for nonexistent workers, salaries and bonuses are ascribed to the accounts of these workers, and even files of directives from the management of the enterprise are compiled. All that is missing is the enterprise itself.

The party leadership of the region, city, or republic, and the police and the public prosecutors—all of whom regularly receive bribes—warn Soviet businessmen in good time of impending inspections. If a commission from the central authorities arrives uninvited, the forewarned dealers set up equipment at the location of the fictitious enterprise and hire people to pose as workers. When after a warm reception the guests depart, their pockets are noticeably swollen, which proves that problems of well-being do not affect everyone in the Soviet Union.[6]

The organization, efficiency, and precision with which underground earnings are distributed stand in sharp contrast to the disorder in social and industrial planning. There is, for example, a smoothly functioning protocol defining the mutual "rights" of city and district secretaries. Thus, for example, when a vacancy which is located within the territory of the district but is a nomenclatura of the city party committee appears, dividends received from bribes connected with filling the vacancy are divided amicably between the secretaries of the city and the district committees. Similarly, in regard to organizations and enterprises on the city level, the secretary of the district committee where they are located obligingly confirms the candidates recommended by the city party organization. Subsequently, when the holder of the city-level position begins to function, he hands over a stipulated portion of the income he receives from black capital to the city committee and to the regional party committee. The Moscow Hotel, located in the Sverdlovsk district of the city of Moscow, may be taken as a case in point. The executives of this hotel (the general manager and restaurant managers) are appointed by the Moscow city party committee, since the hotel is considered to have both district and city-level significance. In other words, the top positions at the Moscow Hotel are "double subordinations," to the district committee and the city committee. Consequently, illegal dividends derived from running the hotel are shared with both district and city party bosses.

There was a time when each party secretary received the money due him directly from each extended hand. Today that money has become anonymous and is collected by a trusted crony, often a relative, who skims off a specified percentage.

Sometimes that person is his wife. V. Tiraskevich, the wife of the first secretary of the Central Committee of the Communist Party of Georgia, was involved in a massive fraud. The front for the dealings of the kings of black capital who directed hundreds of underground enterprises in the country, she received cash and "diamonds of enormous value." Not everything, however, can be acquired for money; for example, rare old books and religious treasures (icons, crosses, silver chalices) cannot be bought. But what cannot be purchased can be stolen, and the accommodating gangsters, who were much indebted to her husband, stole them for Madame Tiraskevich. In the process, some items of value reached the KGB, siphoned off into the hands of top officials, who were obedient puppets of her husband, the secretary.[7] Protected from exposure by the shadow of his wife, the party secretary can play innocent and can, if useful, manifest firmness and integrity.

While the unofficial yearly incomes of the secretaries of the provincial, territorial, republic, and all-Union committees are undoubtedly measured in five- and six-digit figures, the secretaries of the Central Committee of the CPSU can take whatever they want. Money means nothing to them. While they have power and position, they have at their disposal forest preserves, dachas, dazzling trips with full entourage, and personal yachts. Their goal is to stay in power as long as possible, and the means to this is not money but fear, blackmail, and intrigue. Still, one must think of one's family, of children and grandchildren. But for this purpose the slightest hint from the secretaries is enough, and the toadies will obligingly come forward with all the money wanted. For those further down, however, money is no trivial thing. It means independence and comfort in old age, and so the greedy hands of secretaries of varying rank gather in bribes, collect villas, and hoard dollars and sterling.

As a result of a palace coup in Georgia in the 1970s an ambitious phalanx of young careerists forced their way into power, crowding, pushing and deposing from the party throne the entrenched group of old bureaucrats sunk head over heels in corruption. A series of exposures followed, and for a moment cracks and fissures appeared in the hypocritical facade of "developed socialism," allowing a glimpse of the characteristic features of the government mafia and underground business.

Several secretaries of the Central Committee were removed on charges of bribery. The third and fourth secretaries committed suicide. The broom of the purge swept through the entire party apparatus: the first secretary of the Kutais party committee, the secretaries of nearly all the regional party committees, and the heads of the police, the attorney general's office, and the KGB were all removed from office. The wave of embezzlement of state property halted for a while, and prices stabilized somewhat.

One should probably not perceive the reforms in Georgia as a sincere effort on behalf of the new party leadership to reestablish legality there. It posed as honest in order to affirm its own power and because this was Moscow's wish. Shevernadze, the new first secretary of the Central Committee of Georgia, happened to be the sort of man who was able to foresee the tendencies coming from Moscow and act accordingly. At one time the Politburo strove to preserve the status quo in the republic, aware that any serious reorganization would carry with it a threat of severe shock. However, the easygoing life-style in Georgia, many of whose people were involved in underground business, coupled with exaggerated stories of the prosperous existence of the Georgians, piqued people in Moscow. Against a background of national poverty and rising prices, the relative prosperity in Georgia elicited envy from the other nationalities. Responding to the danger of a massive outburst of public indignation, the central Moscow authorities ordered the dismantling of the underground enterprises which had been built up over the years in Georgia.

However, corruption in Georgia (and not only there) had reached such proportions that the measures taken to combat it paradoxically contributed to fostering it. This occurred because the illicit enterprises in Georgia not only were the basis of the prosperity enjoyed by the Georgians but also supplied the national market with otherwise scarce or even unavailable goods. It could be said that these enterprises served the socialist government by eliminating bottlenecks in socialist production and supply. After the KGB attack on black business brought the activities of many underground enterprises to a halt, goods and products that had been readily available began to disappear from the store shelves. The consequence was that the bribe scale was upped, ostensibly to cover the added risk. Moreover, the underground millionaires whose businesses were shut down were forced to continue paying bribes to the high leadership—in order not to be arrested.[8]

The scandalous disclosures did not involve the first secretary of the Central Committee of the Communist Party of Georgia, Mzhavanadze. He was given the opportunity to slip quietly into oblivion; his name ceased to be mentioned, as though he had never existed. Secretaries at this level who are removed from office by a quirk of fate or by a periodic anticorruption campaign are never fully exposed. The style of their leadership, sometimes their performance on the job, less frequently the "survivals of nationalism" they might display—all such shortcomings are singled out for criticism and denunciation, but never their weakness for money, their venality—at any rate, not publicly. Thus it was with Mzhavanadze in Georgia and Akhundov in Azerbaijan, and thus it would be with any first secretary of the Central Committee of a republic. This sphere of their activity is exempted from public censure because they do not simply occupy a post; their position of first secretary symbolizes the party itself, and the party in the USSR is assumed to be wise, just, and honorable. Another consideration, more mercantile than ideological, also prevents public exposure of first secretaries: the need to ensure that the position preserves its potential—for exploitation. Thus corruption in the USSR is free to continue basically unhindered.

Having sketched something of the income of partocrats, we wonder whether we will be believed. However, one cannot base one's understanding of Soviet society on the declarations of Soviet leaders, on publications meant for general consumption, or on official Soviet data or on TASS communiqués. To gain an appreciation of the pervasive character of corruption in the USSR, it is necessary to have lived in the USSR, to have sat in party offices, to have been witness to the making of political decisions. Armchair scholarship has as much in common with Soviet reality as diagrams do with life or as an anatomical description does with a living person.

Notes

1. "According to the amount of goods one can obtain, one Soviet ruble is worth no less than dozens of rubles in the open system" (A. Fedoseev, *Zapadnya* [The Trap] [Frankfurt am Main: Possev Verlag, 1976], p. 303).

2. "In many government agencies the higher-ups are rewarded with what are known as 'special distribution,' actually passes granting them access to special stores located on the premises. Each official, one bureaucrat told me, has some specified quota of money that he can spend in the store, marked on an identification card and fixed according to his rank" (H. Smith, *The Russians,* [London: Sphere Books, 1976], pp. 43–44).

3. "Tucked away on the third floor of G.U.M., Moscow's main department store, is Section 100, a specially stocked clothing shop for part of the elite. In the basement of Voyentorg (a store for military personnel on Kalinin Prospekt) there is a secret shop for military officers. Dotted around Moscow are tailors, hairdressers, launderers, cleaners, picture framers, and other retail outlets . . . serving a select clientele" (ibid., p. 44).

4. "In the Kremlin hospitals, they spend almost one hundred times more per patient than in the Lopatkino clinics, for example, or in ordinary hospitals" (A. Fedoseev, in *Posev* [Frankfurt am Main: Possev Verlag, 1973], p. 113). See also *Cancer Ward* by Alexander Solzhenitsyn, trans. Nicholas Bethell and David Burg (New York: Bantam Books, 1972), pp. 1–2: "Unforeseen and unprepared for, the disease had come upon him, a happy man with few cares, like a gale in the space of two weeks. But Pavel Nikolevevich was tormented, no less than by the disease itself, by having to enter the clinic as an ordinary patient, just like anyone else. He could hardly remember when he had been in a public hospital last, it was so long ago. Telephone calls had been made, to Evgeny Semënovich, Shendyapin, and Ulmasbaev, and they rang other people to find out if there were not any VIP wards in the clinic, or whether some small room could not be converted, just for a short time, into a special ward. But the clinic was so cramped for space that nothing could be done. The only success he had managed to

achieve through the head doctor was to bypass the waiting room, the public bath and a change of clothing."

5. This composite picture of Soviet crime is based on wide readings of several sources of the Russian-language émigré press of the 1970s, e.g., the West German *Posev,* the U.S.-based *Novoe russkoe slovo,* and the French-based *Russkaya mysl',* along with information gleaned from the "central" Soviet newspapers *Pravda* and *Izvestiya* in 1982, 1983, and 1984. A further source was sociological interviews conducted by the author in Israel and the United States in 1982 and 1983.

6. Ibid.

7. Ibid.

8. Fedoseev, *Zapadnya,* p. 299: "At the very pinnacle of power the administrators generally do not have an established salary. They have a so-called open current account, which has no limits at all. In other words, their 'salary' depends on what they want to have." We agree that the people who have power in the USSR—those whom Fedoseev calls "administrators," can have as much as they "want." But they take what they want and as much as they want from the bottomless reservoir of black business. Black business exists, in fact, because its existence in the country is useful and necessary to the ruling class, for the satisfaction of its endless needs. As for the salary of the "administrator," it is very high by USSR standards, but it does have limits. The fact that members of the Politburo receive enormous sums of money for all sorts of meetings and dinners is something else again. And it is impossible to determine which receptions are arranged for the benefit of the government and which are for the administrator's own pleasure.

Chapter 3

The Structure of the Communist Ruling Class

Were it not for a small group of uncouth, fanatical Bolsheviks who rose to power on the crest of the Communist Revolution, it could be said that the Marxists are ordinary obsequious bureaucrats, guided by only one passion—the desire for comfort and prosperity.

Despite the wishes of the Marxists, the liquidation of private property did not lead to a classless society in the USSR (or for that matter in any other communist country). What emerged instead, substituting for the nobility and bourgeoisie, was a new ruling class possessing all the features of a ruling class: power, property, and a privileged position in society. Milovan Djilas defines it as a *new class*, the novelty being its having emerged on the crest of the proletarian revolution. Yet this definition gives little indication of the social location and function of the class. Mikhail Voslensky proposes the term *nomenclatura*.[1] Another possible term is *ideocracy*, which stresses the link with Marxist-Leninist ideology. But these functional definitions only partially reveal the social role and political purpose of this new class in Soviety society. For this reason I propose to use the term *Communist ruling class* to stress both its leading role in Soviet society and its link with communist ideology.

The social origins of the Communist ruling class are diverse. That particular declassed human material which participated in the Communist Revolution came from a number of adjacent classes: the proletariat, the peasantry, and the intelligentsia. At times the proletariat did enter the social base of the Communist class, but sometimes it was excluded, depending on the historical and national features of a particular communist country. Indeed, the attitude of the Communist ruling class toward the proletariat went through various stages. In the period of struggle, during their avowed attack on capitalism, the Communists were forced to rely on capital's creature and antithesis—the proletariat. The appeal to the interests of the working class was a convenient screen for masking the self-seeking efforts of the class that was forcing its way to power. During the interim period, after the bourgeoisie and the nobility had lost power and before the new dominant class had assumed it, a social illusion was created to the effect that the interests of this new class and the proletariat coincided. During this brief period, lasting less than a year—from the middle of 1917 to the beginning of 1918— the toiling masses enjoyed a significant degree of equality and a certain degree of freedom. But as soon as the Communist ruling class came to power and usurped the people's wealth, it found it was not really necessary to act in the name of the people. All that remained of the dictatorship of the proletariat were masks, concealing new communist forms of exploitation. The foundations of the economic power of the ruling class were established by instituting compulsory industrialization and forced collectivization. This brought the inherent contradictions between the workers and the Communist authorities to a point of sharp antagonism; a refusal to comply with the special form of slave relations developed in industrial enterprises and collective farms was cruelly punished. The political goals of the new Communist class were realized by monopolistic domination over economics, ideology, and culture. This resulted in conflict with the so-called proletarian intelligentsia which emerged in the wake of the Communist Revolution and later, in the 1920s and the beginning of the 1930s, in a struggle with the Communist Party itself, which had once given its blessing to the emergence of the ruling class and had ideologically determined its existence.

Nevertheless, the opinion which stated that "to the degree that the new dominant class becomes a force and acquires a more specific character, the role of the party as such will weaken"[2] was not fully justified. What actually weakened was not party control as such but the meaning of the party, the aims and aspirations of which were subjected to the aims of the Communist class. It was the fate of the party that led Russia to revolution to be destroyed in Stalinist camps as soon as its ideals came into conflict with the objectives of the Communist class. The influence of the new party created in the 1930s by Stalin on the ruins of the old Bolshevik party (preserving its identity in name only and consisting in large part of representatives of the new ruling class) inevitably increased and intensified in proportion to the social differentiation of Communist society.

All ruling classes of the past achieved power after economic relations in society reached a certain point of development. The Communist class broke the usual chain of events. First it seized political power, and only later did it lay the foundations of its economic power. However, although the formation of the economic bases of the Communist class became possible only with the victory of the Bolshevik revolution, ideologically this class was formed long before this, though again, without roots or sources in the life of the common people. In other words, the emergence of the Communist class was the product of ideological propaganda and agitation for the realization of the theory of revolutionary Marxism, within which the idea of a Communist class clearly played a primary role. An impression was thus created that the new ruling class originated in the Communist Party and "could have emerged only as an organization of a certain type, distinguished by a special discipline and based on a unity of views and convictions which was obligatory for all its members."[3]

The process of emergence of the Communist class, however, was not the product of a conscious will or a realization of a conscious goal. Its establishment was an objective outcome of the same social conditions that first led Russia to the Bolshevik revolution and then made it a communist country. The Communist class took shape in the matrix of the social and economic life of Soviet society, but the Communist Party was the core around which the Communist class crystallized. The Communist class was the result of the transformation of a group of professional revolutionaries into a group of property owners. The essential goals of this class are not dictated and defined by party statutes but instead derive from its social status and the desire to consolidate and preserve privilege. As for Marxist ideals, their function is purely ornamental, intended to dazzle the masses. The Communist leaders have turned from revolutionaries into reactionaries, as might be expected of a ruling class firmly entrenched in power.

The Communist Party is broader in scope than the Communist class, yet it does not include all the social groupings constituting the ruling class. In and of itself, membership in the Communist Party does not place a person in the circles of the ruling class, nor does it give him either material benefits or privileges. Many millions within the party are no less deprived of their rights than tens of millions of Soviet citizens outside it. Membership in the party does, however, serve as a certain proof of a person's loyalty with regard to the regime.

Some are in the party because instructions were received to accept a certain number of workers, peasants, and intelligentsia, in accordance with Communist Party regulations. Some of these were good workers, some did well in their studies, some were skillful teachers. Offered membership by their superiors, they could hardly refuse: the question might always be asked why the "supreme" confidence shown in them was not accepted. It is by no means easy to find a convincing explanation, since according to ideological postulates the party is the mind, conscience, and so on, of the epoch. If an explanation is not found, the person is denied not only confidence but also a life of peace for many years hence. So Soviet citizens enter the party, painfully aware that from this time on they will have to spend many hours at meetings and performing the work required of a party member. They are not asked about their ideology or ideals—something not found at the top of the party pyramid either, although in rare cases, at the time of one's reception into the party, a certain interest is displayed in one's knowledge of the history of the communist movement or of the international situation.

Another category of people are in the party as a necessary correlative of their position. Every important position in the USSR is bound to a specific rung in the party hierarchy: a minister is required to be a member or candidate member of the Central Committee of the Communist Party, the head of an important board or trust, or a member of a regional committee, while a chief engineer, leading designer, prominent scientist, or outstanding production worker is expected at the very least to be a party member, not only if he wants to advance his career but even if he wants to retain his position.

It stands to reason that there are a large number of people who entered the party motivated by careerism and ambition. But the party membership they hold is not in and of itself a ticket of admission to the upper class. Years are needed for such a person to demonstrate his worth and recommend himself to his superiors. Only then will the barrier separating the Communist class from the masses be lowered a bit before him at this point to give him access to the benefits of membership.

The party is the filter for the selection of candidates for the ruling class, a "purgatory" through which they must pass, abandoning along the way all opinions and independent judgments of their own. It is not correct that "all that is necessary for advancement is wholehearted devotion to the party,"[4] nor is it correct that "never before and in no other place has the way been so open to those who are devoted and loyal as it is under Communism."[5] Wholehearted devotion to the Communist class is necessary, and loyalty is highly regarded, but these are hardly sufficient.

In no society has upward movement into the Communist class been so difficult, and never has it demanded so many sacrifices, as under the Soviet regime. The elitist Communist class is closed off by a barrier as difficult to penetrate as the great wall of China. That only party members can engage in public and political activity or become leaders, diplomats, or employees in the areas of security or foreign trade has created an illusion that membership in the party is in itself a source of privilege, power, and influence. Such a view substitutes the appearance of Soviet social processes for their essence and represents a level of understanding fully in accord with that which Soviet propaganda tries to create among the Soviet citizenry.

"The party cell," writes Djilas, "has expanded to such an extent, that it has begun fulfilling all the main functions of the government. As a result, the party cell as such has disappeared, and all these functions have passed into the sphere of party activity."[6] It is true that communism does not acknowledge a difference between the work of governmental organizations and party institutions. However, it does so not in the sense that the party and the government are largely integrated[7] but in the sense that party and government institutions, the police and science, are *all* dominated by the Communist class, which is nominally connected with the party, its statutes and program, by tradition and propaganda goals. Tribute is paid to ideology only in that the most powerful of the Communist class of the partocrats (the party elite) formally acts in the name of the party, identifying itself with it or, more accurately, identifying the party with itself.

The Communist class is composed of specific social strata which, because of their positions, have exclusive rights to own and dispose of property expropriated by the ruling class and who, with their extraordinary privileges, monopolize the governing of the country. The Communist class has concentrated power in its hands and is unwilling to share it with anyone; indeed, it has no reliable allies in the other classes. Unshared, its power is virtually absolute. It arbitrarily distributes the national income, establishes wage rates in accordance with its own interests, and determines and governs the economic development of the country according to its egoistic requirements. Communist ideology, having given a monopoly on the right to act in the name of all workers to a new class which did not possess private property, allowed that class to dispose of national state property. In this right lies the strength of the Communist class. The monopoly of power of this class was affirmed and expressed in its monopoly on property.

Western experts have tried on various occasions to determine the numerical strength of the Communist class of Soviet society, estimating it at about one million people, and if their families are added, several millions.[8] It is my view that the Communist class, encompassing elite circles in the army, the police, science, and art, far exceeds one million.

At the time of the Twenty-fifth Congress, the Soviet Communist Party numbered slightly more than 15 million members (15,058,017).[9] Of this number, 8.6 percent (ca. 1,295,000) were in the organs of government and economic leadership or in the apparatus of party and public organizations. This is the party-government and social-political elite of the Communist class. To avoid inflating the total, I suggest lowering this figure by 100,000 (the number of technical personnel of the party-government apparatus) and arriving at the figure for the party-government elite of 1,195,000 people.

Of the total membership of the Soviet Communist Party, 4.3 percent work in science and 12.4 percent work in institutions of higher learning, the health professions, culture, and art. While certainly not all the party members working in the above areas are part of the ruling class, a substantial portion of the scientists, educators, and cultural figures to whom the CPSU opens its doors represent the privileged layers of the population: they either occupy prestigious positions or will eventually occupy them. The Communist regime very much wants to win over to its side scientific and ideological workers, as well as physicians who have received public recognition. Thus, there are solid grounds for considering a third of these as members of the privileged strata of the Communist class. That adds another 840,000 people.

About three-quarters (74.7 percent)[10] of all Soviet Communists work in the fields of material production, transportation, trade, public food services, housing, and utilities, as well as on state and collective farms. Sifting out the representatives of the ruling class from this heterogeneous mass is difficult. Very often a party member in a plant or in agriculture is a simple worker. Even if he becomes a unit- or field-team head, he is as far from the elite as a factory foreman or an ordinary engineer. But party members who are directors of industrial plants, construction chiefs, trust and agricultural board managers, chairmen of collective and state farms, or their assistants certainly should be included within the elite strata. In all likelihood, anywhere from 5 percent to 10 percent of party members in the above-mentioned sectors are part of the elite. We have adopted the higher estimate (10 percent) but at the same time have included within it the closely guarded secret number of Communists in KGB, military, and police elites.[11] This adds another 1,125,000 people to my count of the Communist class, which I see as being comprised of 1,195,000 employees in the party-government apparatus, 840,000 workers in science, ideology, health, and the arts, and 1,125,000 workers in industry, agriculture, the service branch, the army, and the police—or a total of 3,160,000 members of the CPSU. If we add to this figure another 10,000–12,000 persons, nonparty members, also within the elite circles of the Communist class (these are in the main from the free professions), we arrive at the approximate figure of 3,170,000 persons defining the circle of the Communist class. Taken together with their families, these "workers" of the ruling class number 10–11 million people. This we consider to be a fairly accurate estimate.

These data relate to 1975, 10 years ago. In the past decade the population of the Soviet Union has increased by approximately 20 percent. Membership in the Communist Party has increased similarly and now reaches more than 10 million. Thus we can posit that membership in the nomenclatura has increased by 20 percent and that at present (including family members) it totals 12–13 million.

In speaking of the Communist ruling class, we have in mind that special group of people, party and government bureaucrats, who have been given power and the numerous cliques who serve and protect them. The diversity of the ruling cliques is conditioned by the fact that the Communist class is required to perform countless functions, more diversified, perhaps, than any other ruling class has known in the course of history. All these cliques participate in the administration of government and society through a complex network of interrelations.

The Communist class is a pyramid comprised of precisely delineated layers. At the top is the party elite, the partocracy. Slightly beneath it is the multilayered governmental elite formed from diverse groups: the Soviet governmental bureaucracy, the military, and the police. Further down, arrayed according to the degree of their influence on the party apparatus and their prestige, are the scientific and trade union elite, the elite of art and literature, and a very small clique of professional public figures.

Superimposed on this vertical gradation, which reflects the degree of participation in the determination of foreign and domestic policy, is a horizontal division representing the interrelatedness and overlapping of various cliques. The highest, most powerful level of the ruling class is formed not only from the partocracy—secretaries of the Central Committee of the party on the national level, and first secretaries of the party committees of the republics—but also draws in representatives of other elite circles: heads of ministries, prosecutors of the Supreme Court, editors-in-chief of the main newspapers, presidents of the academies of science, top generals, and chairmen of unions of writers, artists, actors, and other free professions. Beneath them are their deputies, who implement Soviet policy—bureaucrats of the new breed, who began their political activity after World War II. This group of high officialdom includes heads of departments of the Central Committee, of the Supreme Soviet, and of the Council of Ministers, Komsomol leaders, trade union chiefs, and deputy ministers.

This last stratum merges into a third, made up of the heads of central governmental economic, industrial, educational, and medical establishments, officials of influential organizations, such as the councils of ministers of the republics, the attorney general's office, the Supreme Court, the KGB on the republic and provincial levels, distinguished Soviet scientists, and writers and artists who have been awarded government prizes and titles. Forming the lowest stratum of the Communist class is a group of people holding posts that confer special status: officials, inspectors, executive organizers of party committees, members of writers' and artists' unions, directors of plants, professors and assistant professors, journalists, and a few representatives of the workers and peasants delegated to the Supreme Soviet and party committees.

There is in the USSR no elite stratum of workers and peasants, at least not as a stable social group. A certain number of workers are, however, promoted to Soviet and party elective organizations. If they remain in these organizations for a long period of time, they are drawn out of the worker-peasant milieu and rise up the social ladder to the level of plant directors or chairmen of collective farms. If they serve only one term, that is, if they do not justify the hopes and confidence invested in them by the Communist class, they are expelled from the elite circles after a few years.

While all these groups making up the Communist class participate to varying degrees in the political life of the country, the power emanates only from the elites of the first level, which rely on the cliques of the second. Actually, not all the elite of the first level participate in determining the political course of the country, but only that part represented in the Central Committee, and sometimes only those in the Politburo of the Central Committee, that is, no more than twenty people. Second-level personnel, even if they sit on the Central Committee, rarely participate actively in decisions involving national issues. Rather, they determine the concrete methods of implementing the political lines developed by the highest-level elite. Functionaries on the third and fourth levels are the ones who actually implement policies. They are, as it were, in training schools, testing their skills in governing the country. The most talented among them are recruited into the higher elites.

The Communist class of Soviet society is organized in accordance with the institution of the nomenclatura. The secrecy of social processes within Soviet society has engendered numerous conjectures about this institution.

The nomenclatura has been referred to as the "nerve center" of the Soviet system, or the "secret roster" or network of those in the ruling bureaucracy who control the most important social positions from which they dominate Soviet life. Actually there is nothing mysterious about the nomenclatura.[12] It is nothing more than a network of positions and posts to which one can be appointed only by permission of the party organizations. The nomenclaturas of the national Central Committee, the Central Committees of the republics, and the territorial, provincial, city, and regional party committees—that is, the appointments controlled by each of these bodies—are distinguished according to the nature of the positions and their social importance and public significance (in other words, according to the degree of power they convey). Within each category of nomenclatura are additional gradations. Thus, the nomenclatura of the national Central Committee can be divided into the nomenclatura of the Politburo, the secretaryship, and the departments. There is an analogous division in the nomenclatura of the republic, provincial, city, and regional party committees.

All political, social, governmental, economic, and scientific positions of any importance are covered by the nomenclatura. This is what permits the party organizations (or, more correctly, the Communist class acting in the name of the party) to place all areas of social life of the Soviet Union under its control. The nomenclatura is the most important tool for achieving the ambitious goals of the Communist class, which are disguised as the will of the party. Thus, while the government, military, economic, scientific, trade union, and other elites possess prestige and broad privileges as well as high status, they are subordinated to the will and purposes of the partocracy and lack political power. It is this lack of political power which most sharply distinguishes them from the partocracy.

Controlling the entire system of job appointments, the partocracy reserves all the most prestigious and responsible posts for itself. For example, the premier, the president of an academy, and the chairman of the all-powerful KGB or of a modest writers' union are all recruited from the ranks of the party elite or, if not, are admitted into its ranks as the bearers of the goals and purposes of the partocracy. Thus the authority for any apportionment of power is invariably in the hands of the partocracy. Earlier, under Lenin, the dictates of the partocracy were carried out under the guise of the rulership of the proletariat; later, under Stalin, they were enforced by police terror. Subsequently, under their heirs—from Khrushchev to the present— they are proclaimed directly without inhibition, without regard for the formal prerogatives of Soviet legislative and executive bodies.

While those who serve the party elite as advisers and assistants (lawyers and philosophers, engineers and historians) temporarily derive power from their position, there is in the USSR only one political group, one social category, that possesses real and sovereign power: the partocratic elite. The members of this group dominate all organizations, ministries, academies, soviets, and courts. They circumvent the constitution, interpret laws, provoke political crises, rule the economy, and restrict the rights and powers of the governmental-bureaucratic, scientific, police, and all other circles of power. Above the government but below the party elite is the Communist Youth League (Komsomol), which does not have independent authority or influence but which serves to provide manpower resources for the party.

It is possible to institute widely publicized trials against partocrats, as was done in Azerbaijan and Georgia, and it is possible to criticize the activities of some of them, but it is not possible to eliminate the partocracy as such from the Soviet system without provoking a radical reorganization, for it is the basis, the very core, of the Communist structure.

Functionaries of the party are answerable for their actions to no one except their peers, neither to the executive nor to the legal authorities. Rather, both of the latter are answerable to them. Partocrats may be alcoholics, drug addicts, or homosexuals, but if their political activity is supported by the party apparatus, if it corresponds to its interests and goals, their position is secure. Devotion to communist ideology can compensate for lack of talent and for administrative, intellectual, and professional incompetence. According to the morality set by the partocracy rather than by any public opinion in the country, if a person serves the Communist class (and if his nationality and social origins are no hindrance) the path to self-aggrandizement often opens before him, while if a person is not sufficiently servile to the partocracy, his life is apt to be made complicated and difficult. In the society where the partocrat rules, social utility and significance are defined in terms of service to the partocracy (although ideology hails this as service to the party), and common sense is defined in terms of obsequiousness that will yield personal success and prosperity.

It is not true, then, as has been postulated, that in the USSR there is the sphere of party life on the one hand and economic, social, and creative spheres on the other. Rather, the decisions made on various levels of the ruling class are all determined and controlled by the party elite, and economic, social, and creative activities are permeated with party spirit and bound by a thousand threads to the activity of the partocracy.

Although in accordance with the accepted hierarchy of positions in the USSR the head of a department of the Central Committee of the party nominally is equal in rank (and salary) to a minister, and a secretary of the Central Committee is nominally equal in rank to a deputy chairman of the Council of Ministers, partocratic status is always higher than its nominal value. Thus, a head of a department of the Central Committee supervises the ministry under his auspices, and a secretary of the Central Committee supervises a group of ministries coming under the purview of the deputy prime minister. This supervision is tantamount to control and direction, even if the minister and the head of a department of the Central Committee are both members or candidates for membership in the Central Committee, that is, have equal party status. The fact that the head of a department of the Central Committee is an official in the party apparatus elevates him above a minister and elevates a secretary of the Central Committee above a deputy prime minister.

When it is essential to raise some minister above a Central Committee department head—the apportionment of positions and arrangement of power within the Soviet hierarchy often require this—there is only one way to do this: by elevating him along party lines, for example, by transferring him from membership in the Central Committee to candidacy or membership in the Politburo. He is then answerable only to the General Secretary of the Central Committee. Then even the prime minister himself does not have the right to issue an order to such a minister, but only to advise him as equal to equal, as one Politburo member to another. Thus, by the position of a minister in the party hierarchy, one can determine whether he has been elevated above the government.

Notes

1. M. Voslensky, *Nomenclatura* (in Russian) (London: Overseas Publications, 1984); Hélène Carrere d'Encausse, *Raskolotaya imperiya* (Breakup of an Empire) (London: Overseas Publications, 1982).

2. Milovan Djilas, *Novy klass* (The New Class) (New York: Praeger Publishers, 1961), p. 55.

3. Ibid., p. 54.
4. Ibid., p. 78.
5. Ibid.
6. Ibid., p. 91.
7. Ibid.
8. See T. H. Rigby, *Communist Party Membership in the USSR, 1917–1967* (Princeton, N.J.: Princeton University Press, 1968), p. 348.
9. *Kommunist* (calendar-guidebook) (Moscow, 1982), pp. 22, 31, 44, 52.
10. Ibid.
11. Ibid.
12. Professor Voslensky's book (note 1, above) is the most fundamental study of the origin, development, and nature of the nomenclatura as a social class.

Chapter 4

The Road to Power

The partocracy hears only its own voice and, deceiving itself, it demands from the people that it participate in the deception.

In the USSR every person must be somebody's man; otherwise he is a nobody.

The road to the top in Soviet society is predetermined in accordance with a specific social program in which talent and abilities count for little. The determining factors are origins, nationality, connections, and money. The road is differentiated also by the nature of the elite class the Soviet person tries to penetrate.

The lowest level of the elite is comprised of performing artists and members of the artistic, literary, and scientific elite. It is relatively open in nature. People are recruited into this level simply according to their natural gifts, talents, and abilities. Nonetheless, initiative and originality are discouraged, while loyalty and an obsequious willingness to serve the ruling class are essential. The next level is the semi-closed circle of the industrial and technical elite. The principle of loyalty plays an even greater role in the criteria for selection as a member of this group; nationality is also an important consideration, as are, to a certain extent, abilities and efficiency. Access is also limited by class origin and party membership. The highest levels—the party, government, military, and police elite—are almost inaccessible. Admission into these groups is greatly affected by social origins and nationality. Talent is not needed to penetrate them; on the contrary, a creative spirit, original thinking, and independent judgment tend to disqualify candidates. Even loyalty is not a sure ticket of admission. This level of the elite is a conglomerate of colorless and industrious but indifferent and unprincipled people.

Between the elite levels, barriers are not wholly impermeable. A certain amount of rising, generally from the third level of the elite through the second to the first, is possible. Reverse movement, from the first level to the third, is also possible although significantly rarer. The top Soviet elite is entirely autonomous and does not tolerate any pressure or influence from without; at the same time, it determines the opportunities of all the other elite groups. Dominating it is the partocratic elite. From time to time the elite purges itself, and those who do not fit its requirements are ejected. The elite then closes ranks and for a time is more homogeneous and cohesive.

Each elite is constituted according to the principle of impregnability. From the point of view of the surrounding nonelite classes, what is seen is cohesion and unity. Once a decision is adopted, the elites present themselves to the rest of the privileged world (as well as to total outsiders) as being ideologically united, even if among themselves they have not succeeded in achieving unity of views and actions. They do so to preserve their privileges and power, to increase their privileges and enhance their power, and to maintain the structural integrity of the totalitarian regime.

The unity of the elites reflects not only the unity of their goals and interests. The elite groups of Soviet society are composed of people so similar in their way of life, education, and views that there is justification for speaking of their psychological similarity, of a specific Soviet elite type. One expression of this uniformity is the ability of the representatives of the elite to replace one another in leadership positions and to cross from one hierarchy to another. The structure of these hierarchies and the system of interrelationships among them to a large extent determine the interrelationships of their leaders. The social significance of the various elites—of all except the chief elite, the partocratic—depends on the concrete stage of development of Soviet society. There were times (almost the entire Stalinist period and the Andropov period) when the police elite competed with the partocratic in the extent of their power and influence on processes of social development. The militarization of the USSR and its aspirations to global politics during Brezhnev's rule led to an increase in the power of the military elite. The growth in their social importance can be explained by the fact that force, not only within the country but also outside it, has become a standard tool of the Communist regime against those who oppose it.

The elite is distinguished by a complicated network of family connections, both horizontally (within elites) and vertically (between elites). In the 1970s, by order of the Central Committee, a study was conducted on the structure of the Soviet family. It was found that among 3,980 families from the city of Yaroslavl which by various criteria could be considered elite of the first, second, or third levels, 2,708 families were related to each other, and 448 families were connected by family ties to elite families outside of Yaroslavl, in Moscow, Kostroma, Vladimir, and Rostov.[1] This was characteristic of other cities in the USSR as well. In Baku, 7,210 elite families were studied: 5,100 were linked by kinship ties, and 1,081 were linked to similarly ranking families in the towns of Kirovobad, Sumgait, and Yerevan.[2]

The following correlation is worth noting. To a great extent among elite families on the first level and to a somewhat lesser extent on the second level, a significant number of the children chose the profession of one of the parents and in time filtered into corresponding elite groups: in Baku, 40 percent; in Yaroslavl, 22 percent; in Yerevan, 37 percent; in Moscow, 21 percent. In elite families of the third level, professional "parent-child" succession was characteristic of families of military officers (49 percent) and in the families of police officials (19 percent). In the families of party officials it was almost nonexistent, 0.9 percent.

Some 28 percent of the children of party officials of the city of Baku chose scientific or educational careers, 22 percent chose careers in the arts, 30 percent chose engineering or technical careers, 16 percent chose diplomatic careers, and 4 percent chose military careers. The comparable figures for Moscow showed a disproportionate interest in diplomatic careers—there evidently existed broad and promising opportunities here—but otherwise the general picture remained the same: the children of party officials seemed to have an aversion toward party-governmental careers. Some 38 percent chose a diplomatic career, 29 percent preferred a scientific career, 23.3 percent chose engineering or technical careers, and 7 percent chose the arts, while only 2 percent decided on the army and only 0.7 percent on the party apparatus.

The study did not reveal conclusive reasons for this avoidance behavior,[3] but other sociological studies confirmed that in families of important party officials, party-governmental work as a profession was not respected, and not only by the children who observed the party-governmental functionary at close range. The parents themselves preferred that their children embark on diplomatic, military, or scientific careers, but certainly not party-government careers.[4] Hardly a single scion of even the members of the Politburo of the Central Committee followed the profession of his father. An exception was the son of the minister of foreign affairs of the USSR, Gromyko, and even he, after working for a period of time in Soviet embassies in England and the United States, abandoned his diplomatic career for one of scholarship. At present he is director of one of the academic institutes of the USSR. As for the children of Chernenko, his son is presently to make his mark in the field of cinema-art, and his daughter works as a senior researcher at the Institute of Marxism-Leninism.

Despite this, it should not be assumed that the parents—the party-governmental officials—are disillusioned with their own posts or experience a feeling of dissatisfaction. Each certainly enjoys the varied advantages and benefits to which his work entitles him. Nevertheless, it is significant that 32 percent of the party-governmental officials questioned in the city of Baku reported that if they could start their professional life over they would choose a different path: science, diplomacy, or engineering. Not one of those surveyed expressed a desire to see his children in the field of party-governmental work.

The Soviet elite tries to isolate its youth from the masses. Although there are no private schools in the USSR, there is an extensive network of specialized schools in which the instruction is conducted in foreign languages, as well as schools for musically, mathematically, and artistically gifted children. Formally they are open to everyone, but in practice the children of the elite comprise the overwhelming majority of the student body: in Baku, 79 percent; in Moscow, 81 percent; in Leningrad, 72 percent; in Kiev, 74 percent; in Tbilisi, 84 percent.[5]

Do these percentages indicate that the requirements for admission to these schools are especially demanding or that specific skills, talents, abilities, and habits are needed? The official curriculums do not corroborate that hypothesis, nor does the formal knowledge acquired in such schools appear to be less broad than that obtainable in other schools. On the other hand, the classes here are smaller, the teaching is of higher quality, the educational equipment is better, and there are excellent gymnastic facilities and often even a swimming pool. Such conditions cannot be created in the Soviet Union for everyone, but they are created for the elite. In essence, it is the parents, not the children, who pass the "entrance examination" to these schools. Children from highly placed families are accepted as a matter of course, but for the children of workers, admission is difficult and limited.

Such schools are the training ground for the future members of upper classes of Soviet society, the place where social unity of the ruling class is forged. Their function for the children of the elite is identical to that of the pervasive system of political education and special training schools which molded their fathers, but the elite schools function on a much more fundamental level. There the differences of social origin of the older-generation ruling class are minimized into insignificance in the members of the future ruling class. Under the influence of these schools, the children of the various elites enter adult life as members of a unified Communist class, appropriately conscious of themselves as the ruling class of Soviet society.

Education in a special school is a distinguishing mark of the way of life of the Soviet elite. At age seven a child from a high-ranking family leaves the kindergartens of the Central Committee, Council of Ministers, or KGB where he was coddled and begins to enjoy the broader privileges to which he is entitled. In the first, second, and subsequent grades, his fondest desires become reality. If he wants to paint, there are experienced artists hired to instruct him; if he wants to act, he can participate in drama circles headed by famous actors; music and sports in-

struction is available with distinguished teachers. Although he is
hardly needy, he receives hot breakfasts and, if he should want,
lunches as well. At the end of the day he is driven home by the
family chauffeur.

Whatever the specifics of his biography, the child invariably
grows up within a charmed circle of elite personages. To take
one example from the large number of basically homogeneous
elite families: the father is a diplomat, his uncle is the assistant
head of the archives of the ministry of foreign affairs, his grand-
father is an official of the Central Committee and a former colonel in the Soviet army, his aunt is a Kremlin psychiatrist, and
her father is the head of a concentration camp for political prisoners (an extremely prestigious position in the USSR); among
the boy's friends are the son of the then chairman of the KGB,
Andropov, and the granddaughter of the minister of foreign affairs, Gromyko. In short, he is the quintessence of the Communist class.[6]

From earliest childhood the family instills in its offspring the
morality and values of the elite. Life, it teaches, is the acquisition and preservation of privilege, property, and social position.
Society is ruled by a small group of people; a worthwhile life is
possible only for those who belong to this circle. It is not enough
to be on the perimeter; the goal should be to make your way into
the center. Although around you there are cruelty and injustice,
to struggle against them or suffer because of them is a futile
waste of time, for it is impossible to eradicate them. If you have
money or status, you will have the opportunity to live as you
like. Friends should be scions of prominent party-government
officials and KGB executives, never the children of such "com-
moners" as physicians, engineers, or workers. The child catches
on quickly. When he makes an acquaintance he asks, "And who
is your father?"[7] The privileged child is taught how to speak,
how to dress, how to eat, how to behave. The main thing is to
hide his own thoughts and to conceal his feelings. These lessons
will serve him well. When he grows up, they will be an important
key to give him access to the ruling class. But after the privileged
child finishes school, and before he starts on his career, it is
important that he obtain a place in a university or an institute.[8]

Generally, gaining admission to institutions of higher learning is difficult.[9] There are a great many more pupils who want higher education than there are places in the universities and institutes. For pupils from the special schools, however, it is no problem at all. These schools are closely connected with the universities, and the majority of their graduates are admitted without having to compete for the available places. Moreover, only in the special schools is the teaching of foreign languages conducted on a high, professional level. For beneficiaries of such teaching, the doors of institutes such as the Institute of Foreign Trade, the Institute of International Relations, and the Diplomatic Academy are open wide. When sociological researchers questioned students accepted in 1971 to the Institute of International Relations, it was found that 312 of them were the children of important party officials, 210 were children of high-level Soviet government bureaucrats, 180 were children of senior officers, and 50 were children of academicians and professors, while only 8 were children of workers and 2 were children of peasants. Another finding worth noting, although not directly related to our topic, is that 78 percent of those registered in this institute in 1971 were Russian, 13 percent were Ukrainian, 7 percent were Belorussian, and 1 percent were representatives of the Baltic republics. Traditionally, Jews and Tatars are not accepted, and the numbers of Moldavians, Tadzhiks, and Uzbeks are severely limited.[10]

The goal of the privileged schools in which the children of the elite study is to produce a self-confident person, convinced that power belongs to him by right, by the right of his social origins. Here the character of the future ruler is formed: arrogant, presumptuous, unprincipled—the type of person needed by those at the apex of Soviet power. The pupils of these schools are linked by common training. They do take care and will take care of each other, if not as equals (how can they be equals when sharing the same school desk there may be the son of an ordinary general and the daughter of a secretary of the Central Committee, or the offspring of a famous writer who is the holder of many prizes and the child of the chairman of a regional executive committee) then at least as people with a great deal in common. Each finds that there is much in his peers' biographies that resembles his own. No matter what he is engaged in, whether at play or at work, when taking the first steps in his career he is always conscious that he must serve the interests of the ruling class. Among these people who have grown up together, personal closeness and affinity are combined with respect for the needs of their comrades as fellow members of the elite who are destined to one day set their country's policy.

A young man from an elite family starts his career with the support of highly prestigious and highly prosperous mother and father, aunts, uncles, brothers and sisters. At the family table he hears the talk of people who are influential and who often are policy-makers themselves. Listening to these conversations, he learns the arts of manipulation and becomes convinced that it is his destiny to be a decision-maker too.

The behind-the-scenes trading for prestigious posts is one of the methods of private cooperation among influential families. Thus the distribution of leadership posts is often a major family concern. Wherever the child of the ruling elites goes, he invariably meets people to whom he is closely linked either through his own family or through the family of his schoolmates. Everywhere he finds support and sympathy. His appearance, habits, and manner mark him as a man of a certain upbringing. His acquaintances and friends guarantee that people of influence, status, and prestige will consider him one of them. He lives in a luxurious home or an elegantly furnished apartment. His clothes, even if sloppy or worn, set him apart from those not of his class. As a rule, they are made by the best tailors or bought abroad. He is invited to elite social occasions of joy and sorrow—to fancy parties and to more modest but still elegant funerals. At these and other social events the final polish is put on his social graces, and his behavior and attitudes are fine-tuned to the requirements of his future role and status.

In this way, graduates of elite schools and institutions of higher education mutually maintain and support their consciousness of belonging to the social stratum of people accustomed to ruling others. After completing schools and universities or institutes, elite children go to work in party committees, ministries, the security organs, or diplomatic work. No matter how far they go, they will never be far from the seats of luxury and power, they will never leave the society of important and influential people. The old comrade network will surround them everywhere. They will travel in a world in which their friends and relatives set policy and influence the character of Soviet society.

Notes

1. See the collection *Struktura sovetskogo obshchestva: Informatsionny byulleten' Instituta sotsial'nykh issledovany AN SSSR* (The Structure of Soviet Society: Information Bulletin of the Institute of Social Research of the Academy of Sciences of the USSR) (Moscow, 1973), pp. 81–82.

2. Ibid., pp. 71–72.

3. Ibid., p. 85.

4. Ibid., pp. 61–65.

5. See N. Savchuk, "O nekotorykh problemakh narodnogo obrazovaniya na sovremennom etape" (On Some Problems of Contemporary Public Education), in *Uchitel' i uchenik* (Teacher and Pupil), photocopy edition of the Academy of Social Sciences faculties in Moscow in December 1972. This problem was also referred to, though less openly, by Chernenko at the June 1983 Plenum of the Central Committee of the CPSU ("Speech of Comrade K. U. Chernenko," *Pravda,* June 17, 1983).

6. See John Barron, *KGB* (Jerusalem, 1978), p. 58; also John Barron, *KGB Today: The Hidden Hand* (London: Hodder and Stoughton, 1984).

7. Ibid.

8. Ibid.

9. There are certain Soviet institutions of higher learning to which it is virtually impossible for school graduates to gain admittance solely on the basis of their knowledge. If they do not have the necessary connections, they need a bribe. This is such an accepted and normative tradition that when bribes are not taken it is considered strange and surprising. On July 6, 1978, the editorial board of the Soviet newspaper *Komsomol'skaya pravda* printed a letter of a certain Komsomol member to the director of the Shchukin Theatrical College. He writes: "Dear Comrade Director, everything that passes between us will remain private. Inform me of your home address, and I will send you an

initial payment of 500 rubles. . . . After the entrance examination I will personally hand you another 500. And after the first course, the same amount. I am a Komsomol member with a good reputation. I have dreamed of becoming an actor since childhood. I await a serious answer." And when the director did not accept the bribe, the natural reaction of the Komsomol member—natural for him and for tens of thousands like him—was: "What, did the amount displease you? Did I offer too little? Well, I can add another 500. Only tell me seriously what you want."

10. See Savchuk, "O nekotorykh problemakh," p. 168.

Chapter 5

The Origin and Education of the Communist Class

To achieve success, a partocrat must shut his eyes or deny his sight, lest he be stirred by doubts.

The Communist class in the USSR has reached the venerable age of pensioner, now approaching seventy, yet the Soviet citizen knows little about its social origins. The mystery might have been clarified by the results of a research project conceived by the Academy of Sciences of the USSR under the pretentious title "The Character and Way of Life of Party Officials." The study, begun in May 1971, had barely gotten off the ground when an order arrived in December to close down the project, transfer the people involved, and shelve the material already gathered. Nonetheless, some incomplete and fragmentary conclusions from the research appeared in a collection published by the Institute of Concrete Social Research in 1972, based on interviews with 18,720 party officials active on the political scene before and after World War II.[1]

Some 44 percent of the parents of the partocrats in the young (30–36) and middle (36–42) age-groups were office workers, 22 percent were engineers and economists, 7 percent were lawyers and teachers, 3 percent were scientific workers, 15 percent were workers, 7 percent were peasants, and 2 percent were workers in other fields. The social origins of partocrats who began their careers in the 1920s and 1930s were radically different: 12 percent came from peasant families, 49 percent came from workers' families, 26 percent came from office workers, 9 percent came from military families, 4 percent came from families of party functionaries, and less than 1 percent came from the intelligentsia.[2]

In the course of decades, the educational level of the party functionary has also undergone a change. In 1922, some 2.7 percent of party officials possessed a higher education;[3] fifty years later the corresponding figure was 87 percent.[4] Possession of a higher education is inversely related to official status: among secretaries of provincial committees, 64 percent have a higher education;[5] among secretaries of city committees, 79 percent; among secretaries of regional committees, 84 percent; and among instructors and inspectors of city and regional committees, 92 percent. These figures are an indication that higher education has become one of the current prerequisites for a party career. What is valued, however, is not any form of higher education but rather that obtained in party or higher party schools or in the Academy of Social Sciences of the Central Committee.[6] Of 18,000 party officials interviewed, 79 percent had received their education in these educational institutions, which, it should be noted, enroll students only on the recommendation of the city or provincial party organizations. This last point helps explain why 66 percent of party officials are the sons of highly placed persons. While people from the lower social strata—workers and peasants—do from time to time gain access to a party career, obtaining a provincial committee recommendation for instruction in the party schools is highly problematic for them. Thus, future rulers are most likely to be people who have belonged to elite circles from birth.

A typical beginning party official in the 1970s* was a man from thirty-five to forty years old, possessing a higher education, who had worked for several years in the Komsomol (60 percent) or in trade union work (25 percent), then had taken a course in the Higher Party School (70 percent) or the Academy of Social Sciences (12 percent) and finally settled into the party apparatus.[7] Over the years he began to move up from an instructor, to inspector, to head of a sector. If by age fifty he had reached the post of assistant head of a department, his upward movement would continue. The zigzags of a party career might lead into the

---

*Because no significant differences are revealed in current information about party officials, the picture of this type in the 1970s applies equally to the 1980s.

apparatus of the Central Committee itself or to provincial or territorial committees. However, if a man reaches fifty without having gained a strong enough foothold in party work, he is given to understand that he would be better to move into the sphere of industry, agriculture, or science.

Although education is important for a party career, it should not be concluded that the higher and more complete the education, the more successful the partocrat will be and the quicker and higher he will rise on the career ladder. While graduation from a university or an institute is almost obligatory, anything beyond that is superfluous and even hinders a party career. Graduates of universities and party schools reach the peak of their careers—as heads of departments of the Central Committee or secretaries of provincial committees or city committees—in about thirty years. Those who earn academic degrees, in eighty-two cases out of one hundred, terminate their party careers by receiving the rank of professor or do not rise higher than heads of sectors or of party committees of the Central Committee. Occasionally a professor does rise to a secretaryship in the Central Committee, but only after having traversed a tortuous path that leads from an academic degree to science, in an academy or university, and thence, via intrigues and machinations, to high party positions. This was the path followed by Secretaries Shepilov, Il'ichev, and Ponomarev.

Some 43 percent of the officials of the apparatus of the Central Committee began their careers as instructors of a city committee: 37 percent were recruited from the provincial committees, 12 percent moved up from the fields of industry and agriculture, and 8 percent came from the armed forces and the KGB.[8] Family ties played a significant role: 39 percent of the officials of the Central Committee had relatives who were executives in the ministry of defense, the Committee on State Security, the ministry of foreign trade, or the ministry of foreign affairs.[9]

Those who work their way into the Communist class from the middle and lower classes through their own efforts and persistence are more creative, dynamic, and functionally more effective, that is, they are able to perform different types of work and administer effectively in various posts, while those who come from high-ranking families are more passive. This, however, does not prevent the latter from advancing rapidly in their careers.[10]

In an attempt to encourage activity useful to the partocracy, Communist propaganda tries to convince the Soviet public that a good education and general cultural development open the way to success, achievements, and honor, but the partocratic world, where unscrupulousness rules, gives the lie to this. There, a well-bred person accustomed to politeness, helpfulness, and rectitude is clearly at a disadvantage. Moreover, the very nature of ascent within the partocracy favors the dilettante, the person willing to forego professionalism in the name of party spirit. This can already be seen on the Komsomol level. However promising a young specialist might be, if he shows an inclination toward a party career he is relieved of his specialist duties and appointed full-time secretary. Henceforth, such a person is kept busy on a treadmill, racing from conference to meeting, from meeting to conference. He has no opportunity to augment his professional education or to raise his cultural level, and in time the specialist loses his professional qualifications. At that point, to keep his head above water, he has no choice but to hold on tenaciously to party work. If he breaks with party work, the road back to industry or science is agonizing, and often tragic. Once he has begun to make his career in the party, he realizes how important it is "not to give himself away," that is, not to reveal independent judgments. From here on, principles will have to be sacrificed in the name of directives.

His party career being the only route left open to him, it is not long before he is fully occupied with intrigues and attempts to maintain an uneasy equilibrium as he balances on the slippery ascent of the pyramid of privilege. What is below and beyond his circle and ambition soon drops out of sight. His knowledge of the life of the common man is now limited to indistinct memories fortified by the misinformation appearing in the newspapers. He prefers not to know more, lest his conscience be awakened.[11]

For this reason it would not be advisable to set one's hopes on a reawakening of moral values among these people. The partocrat's appeals to virtue, justice, national suffering, or even national interest are meaningless. His logic is that of a man who follows his own impulses. His only authority—except for his superiors, of course—is himself. He is totally unaccountable to public opinion—it does not exist as such in the USSR. His past, his psyche, his own motives, are the only determining factors affecting the human destinies in his power. Only the partocrat makes decisions: he is the strategist, his subordinates are only implementers. Under these circumstances, politics becomes psychology, and social development becomes a process determined by the unpredictable motives of a single personality or a number of personalities like his.

Nonetheless, the possibility cannot be discounted that to suit his subjective interests some party official might seek to restore human values, as, for example, in the struggle for power during the events of the Prague Spring (1968). Most of the Czech party functionaries demanding reform were motivated by the desire for power. The young partocrats were disturbed by the broad powers of President Novotny and their own lack of power. The inconsistency and indecisiveness displayed by Dubček and his colleagues arose from the contradiction between the self-seeking goals of the ambitious partocrats and the magnitude of the social forces awakened by the Prague Spring. This contradiction will certainly influence "neo-Dubčekites" of the future. Similarly, the nature, and especially the strength, of pressure by the masses on the political leaders may determine certain moves of the Communist authorities during crises and social conflicts. Both Dubčekites and neo-Dubčekites, being spiritually subjugated to communist ideology, are able to create and produce only "morbid" social movements and developments. Therefore a genuine revolution may rely on them initially, only—after a certain period of time (and this is a condition of the utmost importance for the progress of society)—to discard them decisively.

But in the USSR, revolution will not occur soon. It did not occur in 1984, as Andrei Amalrik imagined.[12] In the Soviet Union a transfer of power has just occurred. The main question now is *of what type* will the new Soviet leaders of the Gorbachev era be—successors to Chernenko or, perhaps, people more receptive to new ideas.

We are inclined to think that the history of Soviet Russia will not follow the traditional path this time. Until Gorbachev consolidates his power, a complex and dramatic struggle for power in the Kremlin is to be expected, but in the final analysis younger political leaders will take over the leadership of the party and the government. These leaders will average fifty to fifty-five years of age, and their biographies will differ from those of the previous leaders of the Politburo. The leaders of the Chernenko Politburo began their careers during the years of the Great Purges, forced collectivization, famine, and World War II. They came to power approximately at age fifty, replacing leaders who were destroyed in the Stalinist labor camps. They succeeded in bringing relative stability to the Soviet regime, insofar as a Communist regime can be stable. Those who replaced Chernenko and will soon replace his colleagues were schoolboys in the 1930s. At the time of World War II they were new recruits. The Stalinist era did not leave moral scars and deep complexes on their souls. It can be assumed that they will be better educated than their predecessors, and more self-confident. It is possible that they will be more modern. They have the experience of personal acquaintanceship with the West, but they will remain prisoners of the communist system, slaves to communist ideology. Therefore they will be forced to be as cautious, as indecisive, and as conservative as their predecessors. The sea of hatred between them and the people will not recede, for the regime they will represent is profoundly antipopular, antiprogressive, and antihuman. But it is possible that the sea itself will be calmer. No essential changes will occur in the tenor of Soviet life. The life of the common man will remain difficult as always, although perhaps less difficult, perhaps more. And this does not even depend on the will of the new Communist leaders. Within the limitations of the communist system, they will lose control entirely over social management, over the productivity of labor and the technology of production, and elemental social forces will dictate the standard of living of the Soviet people.

The Soviet elite will continue to enjoy numerous material privileges and advantages, as it does now. The police apparatus will continue to punish viciously (maybe less than now, maybe more; everything depends on the situation of the moment) those who demand freedom, justice, and equality. Important officials will certainly travel abroad more, for the ties with the West cannot be completely broken off. Their leisure activities will become more varied and perhaps more dazzling. They will be patterned after models from the Western entertainment industry. But the working man will work even harder and even longer. Even more tired, he will stand for hours in lines. For the common people, no changes for the better are foreseen: simple workers, as always, will split the cost of a bottle of vodka three ways and drink it with pickles, will discuss and condemn the moral conduct of their neighbors and bosses, will marry not for the first time and divorce not for the last time, will argue about justice and about rights. And they will wait. And hope. And believe in the "bright future."

Because they do not understand the Soviet Union, people in the West pose the unanswerable question: How can it be that on the highest level of Soviet power—in the Central Committee, the Politburo, and the Council of Ministers—the rulers do not understand that totalitarianism is antinational, antipopular, and antihuman? How can it be that what seem to be thinking people—secretaries of the Central Committee, ministers, and generals—do not see the necessity for social reform? It cannot be that they do not love their people; it cannot be that they do not think of its future. In this approach to Russia there are not one but three mistakes. First, partocratic selection does not raise clever people to the oligarchic heights. Second, these people, the members of the ruling class in the USSR, did not receive an adequate education and they perceive reality through the prism of their own interests. Third, no feelings are involved, including love for the people; there is only talk about feelings, and only about one's own feelings at that. If twinges of conscience begin to appear, they are exorcised by fear and punishment.

Notes

1. See the collection *Partiyny rabotnik—sotsiologichesky portret* (The Party Worker—A Sociological Portrait) by the Institute of Con-

crete Social Research and the Academy of Social Sciences (Moscow, 1972), pp. 31–33.

2. Ibid., pp. 18–19.

3. Ibid., p. 24.

4. Ibid., pp. 24–25.

5. Ibid., p. 101.

6. Eyewitness testimony: "The Institute of International Relations demands a reference from the Komsomol from each candidate. The more outstanding the reference, the better the chances for the candidate. His father [the father of the privileged child] phoned his friend, who was at that time the secretary of the Moscow Komsomol City Committee. A short discussion about a portable RCA television took place. As a result, this secretary wrote a reference in which Sakharov [the privileged child] was described as an honest, sincere Leninist and a genuine Communist youth" (J. Barron, *KGB* [Jerusalem, 1978], p. 60).

7. See *Partiyny rabotnik*, pp. 51, 57, 64.

8. Ibid., p. 121.

9. Ibid., p. 24.

10. Ibid., p. 131.

11. The opinion of a former representative of the Soviet elite about himself: "He was compelled from childhood to remember the class to which he belonged; he avoided those who were lower than he was on the social ladder. . . . He did not have friends outside the walls of the institute. . . . He preferred even to travel by taxi, instead of the metro, so as not to mix and not to become part of the crowd. . . . He truly did not socialize with common people" (Barron, *KGB*, p. 61).

12. Andrei Amalrik, the late Soviet dissident and author of the widely known book *Will the Soviet Union Survive Until 1984?*

Chapter 6

The Self-Affirmation of the Communist Class

The main thing that differentiates the partocrat from other public figures is the amount of work he puts into his own career.

The prosperous life of the Communist class does not guarantee its peaceful existence. Fear of making a false move haunts the party official at every step. To deal with, if not to allay, that anxiety, the partocrat constantly needs external confirmation of his extraordinary worth. This need is obligingly met by the Communist regime.

The distribution of status symbols is a complex affair directly related to the real rather than the formal importance of a position. It thus becomes a key to understanding relative positions. The head of a department of the Central Committee, for example, is clearly lower in importance within the apparatus than an assistant to the first secretary, even though the assistant (in contrast to the department head) is not a deputy of the Supreme Soviet or a member of the Central Committee. Moreover, within the Central Committee, the various secretaries have various standings: the secretaries in charge of cadres or those who supervise the army are very high-ranking officials, while the secretary for science is of lesser rank. Thus the importance of a party personage cannot be determined simply by mastering the charter of the Communist Party. One needs other criteria which are more reliable and concrete. I would propose as a key for understanding this problem the criterion of the partocrat's office.

The significance of the party official can best be determined by the nature and size of his offices. All other symbols are of secondary importance. It is obvious that a splendid automobile, "Chaika," which costs the government tens of thousands per year in upkeep, could not possibly be at the disposal of an official with a small office, one not equipped with a government "Vertushka" telephone.[1] As for the elegant limousine "ZIL-114" (5 meters, 78 centimeters in length, with 300 horsepower, wood interior, air conditioner, telephone, stereo and television, bullet-proof glass, etc.), it is clear that the man who rides in it possesses an office the size of a ballroom, equipped, of course, with a high-frequency telephone.[2]

Less important party functionaries (inspectors, officials, executive organizers of the Central Committee) are distinguished by the absence of carpets in their offices and the draperies on their windows; they have nylon curtains or jalousie blinds. Important party leaders (heads of sectors of the Central Committee, leaders of lecture groups, etc.) can be identified by wall-to-wall carpeting, velvet drapes extending to the window sills, and a television in the office. Very important party officials have hand-loomed carpets and desks of mahogany, an indication of higher position than a walnut desk, which in turn indicates a more substantial rank than an oak or metal desk. Their offices come with an additional room for rest; there the official may relax after a tense day, drink a cup or two of coffee, and take a nap. Antique furniture is a sure sign that its possessor is no less than a secretary of the Central Committee.

The nature of the office of the General Secretary is a state secret but reliable eyewitnesses report that in addition to his office there are peripheral rooms with a staff of doctors, bodyguards, and food tasters. Most noteworthy is the length of the General Secretary's office. While the visitor is approaching the General Secretary, he has time to break out in more than one sweat and to be assailed by a host of doubts. This was what was intended. As for the General Secretary, he is able not only to examine the person called to report to him but even to compose, during the time of the guest's approach, a speech appropriate to whatever matter is at hand.

The General Secretary has not one but several offices. One is his working office in the Central Committee of the CPSU in which business conferences take place. It is the largest and most impressive in the Kremlin, with antique porcelain, marble statues, and original paintings. Hundreds of guests can be accommodated therein. Another is for official receptions for foreign guests. This office is decorated with severe simplicity and is supposed to testify to the accessibility and humanity of the Communist leader, to his closeness to the people, to the democratic nature of his rule, and so on and so forth. It is small, and its walls are covered with modest silken wallpaper and heavy but simple draperies. In a glass showcase one may see a banner—a "gift" from the toiling masses to the "beloved leader." On the simple desk covered in plain cloth is nothing personal— papers, a few favorite books: Lenin (a testimony to the firm ideological allegiance of the man who occupies the office) and a volume or two by foreign authors (proof of the breadth of his interests). And of course there are telephones, first a telephone installation with some fifty buttons: one touch of the buttons and he is connected with any Soviet republic or with any ministry. Next to this, under a transparent cover, is a red telephone for direct calls to the President of the United States. There is another telephone for urgent calls to the command of the armies of the Warsaw bloc countries. And naturally, a "Vertushka" and a high-frequency telephone.[3]

The offices of important party officials are luxuriously appointed. In this case, as in many others, the more dubious the essence, the more important the appearance. However, the niceties of good form are not always maintained. The secretary of one regional party committee trimmed his office in teak paneling, which is permitted only in the palatial offices of the secretary of the city committee. Another secretary decorated his premises with paintings of a famous artist requisitioned for this purpose from the local museum.[4]

The exaggerated use of these signs of distinction is unnecessary snobbishness which aggravates undesirable (for the authorities) competition among party officials and gives rise to antagonism and envy. But the most unpleasant consequence is for the visitor. He is bewildered, at a loss to know to whom he has been summoned—to the first secretary, to an ordinary secretary, or to an assistant secretary of a party committee. This is why there is a tendency to bestow symbols of high position only from above.

There is, of course, the possibility that some bureaucrat who has lost his sense of proportion will overstep the boundaries and acquire office furnishings not befitting his station: he is entitled to a Romanian cabinet but buys a Finnish one, or he suddenly orders a marble sink for the personal lavatory attached to his office instead of the cast-iron one allotted to him. This is what happens with those executives whose self-esteem outstrips their status.

At the same time, so that the partocrats do not have the slightest doubt about their own worth, the Communist class bestows on its minions other signs, usually governmental, of social distinction.

At the level of the regional committee, a party official is invariably a deputy of a regional soviet; a department head is a deputy of a city soviet; a secretary is, at the least, deputy of a provincial soviet. But the most desirable position is deputy of the Supreme Soviet. What is essential is not the mere 50–100 rubles per month addition to salary (a party functionary even on the regional level does not lack money) but the fact that the deputy wears a tiny flag on his coat lapel. That gold flag on a red enamel background, the envy of all who do not possess one, bestows on its wearer the right to be served out of turn everywhere—in movie theaters, in public baths, at train stations, in restaurants. In all public places there is the following practice: deputies of the Supreme Soviet are admitted (served, provided for, satisfied) out of turn. Not a single Soviet executive stands in line anywhere. It means a great deal in the Soviet Union to have the right to announce arrogantly, pushing aside the gray, tired mass of workers, "Excuse me, Comrade, it is my right," and, condescendingly showing one's chest adorned with the deputy's flag, to pass through out of turn. The reaction is typically Soviet: the surrounding crowd moves out of the way—"it is his right." In 1970 the significance of the flags of the deputies was nearly destroyed. Flags of slightly different design began to be distributed to all sorts of deputies: territorial, provincial, city, regional, and even deputies of the village workers' soviets, but the public was quick to learn which flags were merely decorative and which were the mark of privilege.

All first secretaries of a city party committee of a large city and heads of departments are, by virtue of their office, deputies of the Supreme Soviet of the USSR: the secretary of a city committee of a provincial town is hardly on a par with the party secretary in a capital city. Since deputation to the Supreme Soviet obfuscates the distinction, another axis of differentiation must come into play, namely, hierarchical distinction within the party. There are candidates for membership and members in the Central Committee, candidates for membership and members of a bureau of the Central Committee, and so on. The selection is made according to very rigid criteria in exact accordance with the position occupied. Some secretaries of city committees (cities with a population of several hundred thousands) are permitted to be members of a republic Central Committee; other secretaries (cities with a population of approximately one million or more) are entitled to membership in the Central Committee of the Communist Party on a national level. At the highest level of the Soviet hierarchy, still another gradation is added—membership in the Politburo of the national Central Committee and membership in the presidium of the Supreme Soviet.

In the USSR every important position is accompanied by representation in prestigious organizations. In the national Central Committee of the party and the Supreme Soviet, 95 percent of all members and candidates for membership in the national Central Committee and its inspection committees are in this party forum ex officio. Membership in the Supreme Soviet is determined according to the same principles. Represented on it are delegates not of the people but rather of the multifaceted specter of the party-governmental apparatus. The Supreme Soviet is the more imposing forum—its deputies number several thousand people, while the Central Committee of the Soviet Communist Party is composed of several hundred people. This is why the Supreme Soviet is used, in part, as window dressing for Communist democracy. In the Central Committee of the party there must be no outsiders. There each member receives his position due to his position and power elsewhere. Furthermore, the Central Committee, in contrast to the Supreme Soviet, possesses real concrete power. It forms the supreme organs of the party and controls its policies. Thus, those of the ruling class whose loyalty has been thoroughly tested are delegated and co-opted to the Central Committee. As for the Supreme Soviet, it neither wields power nor rules, and it contains a certain (even significant) percentage of workers, a required number of collective farm laborers, and a sprinkling of intelligentsia and of course of women—"modest workers for socialist construction." None of these forms a competent body; they are extras who pass through their terms as deputies without influence and without leaving a trace. All decisions are made only by those who are entitled to be in the Supreme Soviet because of their positions. The function of the rest is to raise and lower their hands at the proper moment during a vote.

A significant portion of the voters in the USSR do not vote, partly because of indifference and apathy (because of their powerlessness and lack of legal rights), but chiefly because elections in the USSR are a falsification, after which everything remains unchanged. There are hundreds of thousands of formally elected positions in the USSR, and many millions of rubles are spent on all sorts of election campaigns. This may be incomprehensible to the reader unfamiliar with communism. Why spend this money, since there is in essence no one to elect in the USSR? For each position there is only one candidate, and even if no one other than the candidate were to vote for himself, he would be elected. Such is the logic of Communist democracy. But the USSR is an ideological society in which it is not reality which determines ideology, but ideology which dictates the style, norms, and rules of public life. The cult of communist ideology is essential to the ruling class, for only by means of this ideology is it somehow able to explain and justify the existing order in the country. The expenses incurred to preserve the outer trappings of democracy, the essence of which has long been obsolete under the Communist regime, are the contribution of ideology.

But the voters vote in their own way—with their feet, away from, not toward the polling places. There are many thousands of polling places and election districts in the country, and attached to each of them is an authorized representative of a party committee whose task is to "ensure" votes. In the first decades of Soviet rule, party propagandists tried to attract the population to elections with snack bars, pleasant surroundings, and performances by amateur entertainers. But although the opportunity to hear a concert or perhaps to buy cheap salami was tempting, the number of voters declined from year to year and the number of activists from party committees sent to mobilize the voters grew larger. In the 1940s, propagandists with ballot boxes were sent around to homes, to each apartment. This was exhausting and troublesome, but it did somehow ensure the voting process—until the voters began to flee their apartments. Then, in the 1960s it was wisely decided to let whoever wants to vote; the voting commissions would in any event turn in the necessary figures. Thus the percentage of those voting in the USSR turned out to be exceedingly high: 99.9 percent. But as such elections became routine, the party leaders responsible for them were unable to distinguish themselves in any way. Ambitious party activists sought a solution. District, provincial, and republic election commissions began to turn in "exemplary" results: in such and such a voting district the voting was entirely completed at five o'clock in the evening, seven hours before the polling place was to close. In another it was completed at four or even three o'clock in the afternoon. But one day, when one city election district in 1970 reported the completion of voting at noon, the higher leadership of the republic was indignant: one had to show some moderation in one's claims. To find out what had happened, they sent an inspector. As it turned out, the voting "business" in the city had been conducted in a surefire manner. The thought of sending out propagandists did not even occur to the chairmen of the polling places. They had serenely played checkers, drunk tea, and from time to time in accordance with the plan on their charts thrown the necessary number of ballots into the ballot box and made out lists of those who were supposed to have voted. At noon the entire voting procedure was completed: 99.98 percent of the ballots had been cast.

Why not 100 percent? There was always a danger that one of the original "voters" might show up—a retired colonel of the militia or a senile special pensioner—and become indignant because he did not receive notice of the election. In such cases a simple scene is acted out. The chairman of the polling place and the authorized representative of the party committee make indignant inquiries: "This cannot be. We have looked at the lists. Everything is in order. Voter so-and-so is on the list and . . . he has already voted" (they voted for him). They calm the excited, indignant "conscientious" citizen and invite him into the office of the chairman of the polling place. A categorical order to find the guilty party ensues, and meanwhile the angry comrade is treated to a glass of cognac. At this point, a sweet young girl, specially prepared for this role, appears. She acts penitent. It seems that by mistake she checked off the wrong voter and mistakenly gave the wrong voter the ballot. She is assailed by a storm of harsh threats. The girl cowers with fear. By this time the conscientious citizen begins to take the part of the unfortunate girl: she is young and inexperienced. He appeals to the chairman: What if we forgive her this first offense? And they forgive, say goodbye, and everyone goes off happy, the citizen convinced he has fulfilled his civic duty, the chairman hopeful that it has blown over, and the girl preparing to meet the next odd voter. The secretary of the Central Committee of Azerbaijan, Guliev, indignantly related the story of this initiative at a session of the active members of the republic party organization in Baku in February 1971. Nevertheless, the lesson of that initiative was widely applied. By the next regular election in many towns in Azerbaijan, it was reported that by two o'clock in the afternoon 98.9 percent of the voters had voted.

Alienation in the USSR is so profound that a person deprived of the external attributes of his existence—his job or his social position—completely disintegrates as an individual. Neither intellect nor training can save him, for in the USSR the value of a person is a function only of the role the government assigns to him. In bestowing outward symbols, the government projects to a person a desired model of behavior as well as a perception of his position by others. This process has developed to such a point and has so thoroughly succeeded that a person, without being conscious of it, is in constant need of external indicators to affirm his existence. Thus people who have been deceived by the government a thousand times respond to decorations and titles, each in his own way, but in strict accordance with the rules of the Soviet game. Other things being equal, a citizen decorated with an order carries more social weight than a citizen who is not, even if the latter is intelligent and the former a fool. This mania for external symbols encompasses all, including ministers and secretaries of the Central Committee.

Another indication of the relative importance of a Soviet official is the period of time during which he may act independently without referring to his superiors for directions. For example, the head of a department of a regional party committee must report to the secretary of the regional committee once a week; the secretary of the regional committee is summoned to report to the secretary of the city committee once a month; the secretary of the city committee makes his report before the provincial secretary, as a rule, once in several months. All those who must report daily are little respected by the government and party apparatus, and their status in the Communist hierarchy is naturally low. Those who work under constant scrutiny and control are at the very bottom of the Soviet official hierarchy.

To the degree that the intervention of the party and the government in people's personal lives is broadening and deepening—as is indeed occurring—the partocracy, like all other categories of officials who act in the name of the government, acquires more influence and importance. A nomenclatura official carries such great authority and weight as precisely fixed in the scale of social prestige that the masses are forced to model themselves after him and to perceive and identify their place in society in comparison with his. Powerful publicity and popularization of their social authority has placed the Communist elite in a strong spotlight. The way of thinking and essential values, views, and ideology of the Soviet ruling class are becoming not only the standard and criterion for behavior but also the required norm of life, departure from which is punished as a crime.

Notes

1. The "Vertushka" is the slang name for a special telephone, part of an autonomous telephone system that is not connected to the city

telephone system. The presence of this telephone is a symbol of high position in Soviet society, exactly like a big office and a personal car with a private chauffeur. Its other name is "sotka" (once there were one hundred ["sotnya"] of these telephones in Moscow; now there are many more). Alexander Yanov, in his book *Detente After Brezhnev: The Domestic Roots of Soviet Foreign Policy,* Policy Papers in International Affairs (Berkeley: Institute of International Studies, 1977), mistakenly identifies the "Vertushka" with the VCh, the high-frequency (vysoko-chastotny) telephone, which is installed in the offices of only the very top leadership: members of the Politburo, secretaries of the Central Committees of the republics, ministers, commanding officers of the army, and so on. This is supposedly the only form of telephone communication not subjected to eavesdropping. We also cannot agree with Yanov's view of this telephone as a symbol of the political domination of the post-Stalin nomenclatura of the Central Committee of the CPSU over the post-Stalin KGB. It was Stalin who initiated the installation of these telephones. His primary goal was to protect the system of governmental communication with the front during the years 1941–1945 from the danger of eavesdropping by the enemy.

2. See note 1.

3. This detailed description of the offices of the General Secretary of the Central Committee is based on various materials leaked to the Western press in the early 1980s by people who had been present in Brezhnev's, Andropov's, or Chernenko's office.

4. This information is based on a sociological inquiry begun in the USSR in 1971 by the author on the topic of "The Way of Life of Party Officials." This research was later continued by the author in Israel. The facts about the tenor of life and habits of the Soviet elite are based on interviews with former Soviet citizens who were repatriated to Israel in the 1970s and early 1980s.

Chapter 7

The Barricades of the Communist Class

If an elite wants to be admired, it must keep the crowd at a distance.

There are many interconnecting threads binding the Communist class into a single-caste pyramid of power: tradition, ritual, and habits formed over decades, and clubs modestly called "houses of culture" without conspicuous signs or emblems. Near the homes of party, government, and other functionaries are located remote government dachas. Behind heavy doors and cut-glass windows, hidden among the foliage, stand detached and impressive mansions. In every town and in every regional center there is at least one such club, camouflaged as a dispensary, a guest house, or even a sauna. These elite clubs play an extremely important role in the life of the country. Final decisions are made in sessions of the Politburo, collegia of the ministries, and bureaus of the provincial, city, and district committees, but preliminary consultations and formulations often occur in the clubs. In a private, relaxed atmosphere key contacts are made. The powerful of the Soviet world—partocrats and technocrats, diplomats and prosecutors, presidents of academies and heads of writers' or artists' unions, in short, those who give and those who carry out the orders—meet here. Here they do not ask for identification; a car with a government number and well-groomed chauffeur serves as a pass. A doorman obsequiously welcomes the guest. The heavy doors swing open before him, and his hat is taken. From that moment on, ritual embraces him. The cuisine is refined and the wine is vintage. The Communist class relaxes here without worry or constraint. There are billiard tables, fine-quality, highly polished pianos, gold candelabra, color television, stereo equipment, and a wide choice of foreign newspapers and magazines not sold on the streets. And for those seeking solitude, there are large, comfortable libraries.

Banners or posters with shrill slogans about the obligations of the vanguard which are obligatory in a workers' club or a factory recreation and reading room do not disturb the refined tastes of the habitués of these "homes." Instead, canvases by famous artists and antique lithographs, not displayed anywhere else, give the elite access to the refined world of art and allow them to develop a feeling for their own importance. And, of course, the very atmosphere of haughty ease created by years of close acquaintance and the informal way of addressing each other proclaims: Here is where a special world—the world of power—begins.

These "homes" or clubs of the Central Committee of the Soviet Communist Party are accessible to only a small circle. They have special rooms for the most-favored secretaries of the Central Committee and members of the Politburo. The provincial committee and city committee homes are more democratic: here representatives of high-ranking intelligentsia, influential people from military circles, industrial managers, and bosses of national security meet.

The connection point and meeting place of representatives of the very highest and the merely high elite are the arts clubs, the "homes" for participants in the arts: writers, journalists, painters, composers. High-level secretaries of the Central Committee drop by these clubs from time to time for "a little diversion," for an experimental play, for a film forbidden by the censors, or simply to socialize with bohemia—to look over a famous film actress, to pair up with an elegant ballerina, to drink a mug of Czech beer with a famous poet who perhaps would write some verses about him. Here all the people are "our crowd." All who belong to this circle are its passionate devotees and defenders. Some of them occasionally permit themselves to express some mild embarrassment, but nobody rejects this world outright. It is the benefactor on which one's well-being rests. Even the partocrats themselves like to criticize it from time to time—only some trivial thing, of course, never the essence. They love irony, although they reject sarcasm; they admire biting epigrams and witty stories. Each person accustomed to such a "home" is also accustomed to a specific way of thinking and standard of behavior, although in the "outside world" each one has his own sphere of influence: one rules a province and another tyrannizes a writers' union.

The clubs, too, have a pecking order. In the more modest ones, those connected with city or district committees, the choice of dishes is limited, although Armenian cognac and salmon are available. There, conversations are based on generally accessible information about the extent of bribe-taking, family gossip, and methods of advancement. The clubs of the Central Committee and the Council of Ministers are different. In these clubs everything is the best quality—the furniture, the table settings, the cuisine. Here it is the thing to discuss the habits and moods of the secretary of the Central Committee or to consider the consequences of government reorganizations. One can meet, at the same table, the attorney general and the minister of internal affairs, the president of the Academy of Sciences and the chairman of the State Planning Committee. The tables sag under the delicacies, the waiters are in snow-white livery. In these clubs, at candlelit suppers, the pyramid of the division of labor in the ruling of Soviet Russia reaches its apex. Here is articulated what afterward will be conveyed along the channels of power: decisions and resolutions of the Central Committee are formulated, interpreted, and analyzed in the clubs, and only then sent out to the masses as political policy. It is true that not every frequenter of such a club is necessarily a political leader. It is also true that this picture is somewhat generalized. Nevertheless, these clubs are clearly nerve centers of influence and power in the country.

The club is composed of a complex and intricate hierarchy. Frequenters of the club are divided into small groups, or cliques. Sometimes there are within these groups political figures who have already been cast from power, who form a kind of background or "Greek chorus" for the still influential and powerful. The clubs perform very specific social functions: (1) Membership in them indicates in whose hands power in the country is concentrated at the moment and who is on what level of power. (2) Specific positions are determined and taken there: support is shown and alliances are made; the scenarios of the ever-changing political intrigues are "written" in these clubs.

To know who holds the reins of power in the USSR today, one needs only to make a list of the names of the regular visitors to these clubs. It is true that occasionally one can see visitors formally not entitled by their status to belong to these clubs—such as shop heads, staff heads of major industrial enterprises, or managers of cooperative units. They look uncomfortable, drink little, and say little. Their presence is a sure sign that some profitable transaction has been completed and that the pleased partocrat has invited this faithful and humble servant out of gratitude, since the clubs are not only the summit of the pyramid of social prestige but also a venue for conducting big business.

In addition, one very often sees in these clubs ambitious ballerinas intent on building their careers, women singers dreaming about "the big time," and women whose main merit is simply their youth and beauty. These clubs may be their road to success. These women display their charms in their bids for help in their careers or for money or for whatever benefits the habitués of this club might provide. They may start with modest advances such as a solo or a dramatic reading in the club, but the culmination will occur in a tryst in a more solitary location. There the partocrat can find relief from his virtuous labors, and the woman can win the reward she is seeking.

Chapter 8

The Personal Life of the Communist Class

> Communism is a theater without an audience, in which the actors applaud each other.

The top Soviet functionary has broad opportunities for free-time activities. When he tires of his professional offices, he can retire to a log cabin in the mountains or seclude himself in a remote government dacha on some azure coast. He can betake himself to an elegant sanatorium or rest home in the middle of a forest. Nevertheless, the entire personal life of an important bureaucrat is predetermined and conventional; there are no more variations and surprises in it than there are in a minuet. The choice of pleasure may be basically limited by his age, but opportunities for enjoyment are also limited by the necessity for keeping his indulgences secret. The range of interests is small: buying up valuable antiques, collecting abstract art, amassing luxurious automobiles.

Certain basic traits characterize the tenor of the lives of Soviet party executives. There are no stable attachments, only relations either with bosses or with inferiors, monotonous work, and emotional fatigue. Because of the monotony of the Soviet lifestyle and the poverty of imagination, time hangs heavy on their hands. Once they leave their luxurious offices they are often tormented by boredom. They have already seen everything and have amused themselves in many ways. They are not surprised by the attention lavished on them; they are used to it. They need never worry about having enough money. They never experience the humiliation of not being recognized, and mendacious compliments and praise are their invariable companions. But they are subject to internal forces, such as the dynamics of ambition. Therefore they constantly seek confirmation of their significance and importance, especially in the accumulation of money. They try to accumulate today more than they can spend tomorrow. They also enjoy tyrannizing others, humiliating those who must deal with them. Despite their pretensions to superiority and singularity, they remain like pre-programmed machines, acting, moving, or interacting with others according to predetermined patterns and programs.

Since their lives are essentially so empty, they find it necessary to conceal the inner emptiness with splendid decorations. This begins, as a rule, with their living quarters, which are not only an example of vanity but also reflect the way the Communist class perceives itself and bolsters its self-esteem.

A big house or apartment means a big man. A small house or shared apartment means an insignificant man. It cannot happen in the USSR that a person unconnected to the Communist class lives in a home like that of a party executive. The appearance and size of a Soviet citizen's apartment are always a function of the nature of his relations with the authorities. Since an apartment cannot be bought but can only be received as a benevolence from the hands of the government, it is an excellent means of putting pressure on a person. Each successful step in one's career is accompanied by a move to a new, more spacious, and more comfortable apartment. Although fancy cars and smart clothes are important for the partocrat's self-image, his living quarters are the main symbol of his dominant status. Personal dachas and villas behind thick wooden fences are considered appropriate, but barriers of barbed wire are even better, for these instill fear in any "commoner" who might catch sight of this protected preserve.

Preservation of social distance is very important in the USSR. From a social point of view, it would be awkward for an important official if he sat down to an overflowing table while a neighbor in the shared apartment—a worker, engineer, or doctor—sat down to canned smoked meat and pickled cabbage. Social distance derives from ideological considerations. If the Soviet party executive is fenced off from the worker by high walls and a well-groomed private garden lies between them, then there is some hope that for a certain period of time the worker will not find out how his leader lives, what he eats, and with whom he meets. In this way the illusion about a society of equal opportunities will be at least partially preserved.

The tendency to isolation, which thus arose out of ideological necessity, is becoming a cult. The top Soviet leader, the General Secretary of the CPSU, may own a five- or six- or seven-room apartment, a relatively modest dwelling for the most powerful person in the Soviet Union. This is his residence for his voting district; here he poses for photographers. Even those who have nowhere to live or who are crowded into a cramped shared apartment appreciate the justice of this situation. "How can I expect better if even the General Secretary himself has only six or seven rooms?" His home seems approachable: it is an ordinary, well-constructed building with an obligatory policeman at the entrance. However, in fact, not a single General Secretary ever really lives in such a flat. He lives in a villa of twenty to thirty rooms usually located in the suburbs of Moscow and surrounded with a three-meter-high fence with a whole army of policemen guarding it. Moreover, this is not his only residence. If a General Secretary feels the urge to hunt, he can travel to Zavidov, a splendid estate 120 kilometers north of Moscow reserved only for him. For rest, he has at his disposal a villa in Oreande in the Crimea and a dacha in Pitsunde on the Black Sea, where conferences with leaders of "fraternal" Communist parties are often held. In addition, he may avail himself of a dozen dachas and cottages in the Caucasus and in the Baltic republics, in the Valday region, and on the Karelian Peninsula.

The other Soviet leaders also have no need to complain when it comes to living quarters. For example, a premier has on Vorob'ev Road a luxurious modern home with a view of the Moscow River. This was the former abode of Kosygin, although he preferred to live in a mansion near Moscow. Premier Tikhonov has two such mansions located in the beautiful suburban locales of Barvikha and Zhukovka on steep hills overlooking the peacefully flowing Moscow River. The premier has summer residences in the Caucasus Mountains and on the shores of the

Crimea, with marble steps descending to the sea, fresh and salt-
water pools, and tropical gardens.

All these palaces, villas, houses, and cabins are isolated from
the outside world by stone fences, massive iron gates, and alarm
systems. They are forbidden zones, their luxury veiled in secrecy. There are few people who have seen these homes, but
even the residences of second-ranking Soviet leaders impress
and overwhelm. Here is a description of one such home:

> The house is located in a fashionable wooded suburb and reminds
> one of the countryseat of a landed gentleman of middle rank. When
> you enter the first, enormous bright room, you find yourself . . . in
> the eighteenth century. Originals by old masters hang on the walls.
> One has to avert one's eyes from the sparkling parquet illuminated
> by a magnificent crystal chandelier. The furniture is a collection of
> wondrous antiques. It is a museum curator's dream. The rows of
> armchairs along the walls make one feel that they should be covered
> with plastic with a sign attached that says "Please don't touch." . . .
> [You then pass through a heavy carved door and enter the next
> room, which is part of the twenty-first century. This is not a room for
> living but rather] a set for shooting a spectacular science-fiction
> film. . . . [Then you descend a narrow little staircase and enter] the
> Middle Ages: Here the walls are of rough unfinished stones and
> decorated with ancient hunting weapons. The furniture and the floor
> are covered with the skins of wild animals; thick, twisted logs hoary
> with age smolder in the tremendous fireplace. The solemn, somber
> chorales of Bach wash over you from an unknown source.[1]

The powerful of the Soviet world do not need their own apartments or homes because the guest houses of the Central Committee and the Council of Soviets are at their disposal.[2] They
may not only use them for guests but also expropriate them for
their own personal use. The present first secretary of the Central
Committee of the Azerbaijan Communist Party, K. Bagirov, like
his predecessor Aliev, attempted to stress his simplicity and
humility by declining to move to the official government residence. Bagirov stayed in his old seven-room apartment in the
center of the city of Baku, in which he had lived when he was
simply a secretary of the Central Committee of the republic.

This was evidently in imitation of Brezhnev, in order to create the myth of the humble man of the people. In fact, the imitation is complete: Bagirov is only registered in that apartment. In reality he lives in one of the guest houses of the Central Committee some distance from the city, in a three-story separate residence of a dozen and a half rooms built in the style of a medieval German baronial castle. A kilometer-long roadway bordered on both sides by exotic plants leads from the gates to the house. The interior of the palace is a replica of the decor of the castle of an Azerbaijani prince.

In recent years there has been a tendency for the ruling class to have apartments in the center of town, camouflaged behind the flat facades of high-rise buildings. In fact, each apartment is a house within a house, with two stories, many rooms, and a private elevator. The apartment has a fireplace and a spiral wooden staircase. In accordance with the tastes of the occupants, walls are taken out and rearranged and the kitchen and bathrooms are remodeled. The rooms in such a home are at least four, five, or six times larger than standard. The living room is fully half the size of a tennis court. Such a mansion, hidden behind an ordinary flat facade of glass and concrete, offers its occupants the maximum in comfort, while externally it is nearly indistinguishable from the mass of run-of-the-mill Soviet apartment buildings. To safeguard the secret of its luxuriousness, the strictest security measures are observed: messengers who deliver the mail have to produce special certificates, and guests are admitted through several guarded entrances only with the permission of the occupants.

Such homes are the last word in Soviet fashion. They are to be found in most major cities: in Moscow on Peace Avenue, in Leningrad on Lenin Street, in Kiev on Kreshchatik Street, in Baku on Lermontov Alley. The interior decor of these apartments is quite impressive: the walls are wood-paneled and hung with expensive paintings and tapestries; the floors are of colored parquet; there are bronze chandeliers and silver and antique statues. When it comes to expense, money is no object. This is the new style of the new Communist ruling class.

Occasionally some of the communist precepts, which the

elites repeat to their inferiors and which they themselves are
supposed to implement, may be recalled by the inhabitants of
these apartments. One such precept of Engels was "Private
property should be abolished; all property should be socialized."
However, the rulers of Soviet society would not be hard-pressed
to find a justification for the luxury they enjoy. Their logic would
be that the ruling elite should not be bothered in public places,
that it would be inappropriate for them to have to deal with
common people and be pestered by their requests and com-
plaints. Thus, if they did not have appropriately isolated apartments, they would have to live like monks instead of lords. The
way things are now, they have a proper place to receive guests,
and outsiders cannot intrude.

Decorous official dinners are arranged for ten to twelve persons as a rule. All the guests are important people. If the secretary of the Central Committee invites guests, they must be of a
rank—like ministers or generals—that will lend the meeting the
appropriate class. If writers are invited, they must be ones who
have received national distinction, such as laureates or major
awards. Members of the bohemian world are not invited; they
might abuse the host's hospitality by letting slip an impolitic bit
of gossip or by making an ironic or otherwise inappropriate re-
mark that would redound to the host's discredit. Thus social
isolation protects social status. The matter is different if one is
organizing a social evening and not an official dinner. At a social
evening—held at suburban dachas without wives or children,
not at official residences—performers may be present. On such
occasions the plutocrats throw aside the burden of the difficult
problems of government, get drunk, and enjoy gypsy singers and
the daring songs of Okudzhava and Vysotsky.

The aspiration of the Communist class toward wealth and luxury has a further aspect, perhaps the most important one. The
Soviet elites view the amassing of fortunes as their most important means of preserving themselves as a class. The peculiar
feature of the Communist ruling class is that it has not been able,
at least until now, to transfer legally its power and privileges to
its children. Such is the limitation imposed upon it by communist
ideology; such is the price of the attempts of the new Soviet

rulers to camouflage their egotistical goals and self-serving policies with this ideology. However, the Communist class is finding a solution to this problem by utilizing academic positions endowed with long-term social status not dependent on the shifts in political tides. The receipt of academic degrees and ranks guarantees a Soviet citizen high social position. According to the constitution of the Academy of Sciences, a corresponding member of the Academy receives a lifetime salary of 350 rubles a month, and a regular member receives 500 rubles a month. Academicians have at their disposal dachas, special private stores, and cars. The fundamental difference between an academician and a partocrat is that the prosperity of the former is less spectacular but more secure. And security is the most desired ideal of Soviet officials exhausted by intrigues and constant dependence on their superiors.

Adzhubei, Khrushchev's son-in-law, lost all his important positions when his father-in-law fell because his power was based only on his high place in the structure of the Soviet partocracy. He lacked the foresight to provide for himself when the power constellation would change and thus neglected to prepare for himself an academic sinecure. More shrewd was Kosygin's son-in-law Gvishiani, who jumped ship in time to become a member of the Academy and could view the future without apprehension. Children of slightly lower-ranking Soviet leaders did the same (or their fathers arranged matters for them). The son of Khrushchev's friend Shelest, head of the Ukrainian Communist Party, made it into the Academy at the very last minute, on the eve of his father's fall. Gromyko's son has not waited; he is a member of the Academy and is comfortably ensconced in the Institute for the Study of Asia and Africa. What one can conclude from such maneuvering is that while the title of academician may not guarantee the intellectual stature of a person, it can guarantee him a peaceful, prosperous life.

The next step in the process of perpetuating privileges is the transformation of lifetime rights into hereditary rights. While position in the party hierarchy is not hereditary (not even a lifetime privilege) and the title of academician cannot be passed on to one's heirs (although it *is* a lifetime privilege), property and valuables can be handed down from father to children to grand-children. Such capital—from property, valuables, and money acquired—fuels the movement of the individual toward power in the USSR. Money guarantees acceptance into an institute and buys a prestigious position that guarantees high status. This status in turn provides opportunities for acquiring money. Thus the Soviet Communist class has finally broken free of the limitations imposed on it by ideology. In capital it has found a universal means for perpetuating its own privileges and influence and for giving its biological heirs the means for acquiring power and becoming its social heirs as well. It has become the ruling class in the full sense of the word, combining a monopoly on property, a monopoly on power, and a monopoly on the perpetuation of power. Its internal dynamics have become circular: social status ⇆ academic status ⇆ capital.

The ruling class has solved another important problem relating to its aristocratization (the preservation of its homogeneity) by interelite marriages. The marriage market is also part of the spiral of power. After a "less appropriate" marriage, Stalin's daughter married the son of the secretary of the Central Committee, Zhdanov; the daughter of Premier Kosygin married the son of KGB general Gvishiani; the son of academician Semenov married the daughter of academician Khariton. Thus a living barrier against penetration of foreign elements is created. From private trips abroad to private villas, from private special schools to private institutes, from a private way of life to endogomous marriages—the boundaries of the Soviet ruling class are kept closed.

Thus there is adequate evidence to show that the Communist class, the ruling class of Soviet society, lives an easy and luxurious life. Is it likely that, having reached the social summits, the Communist class finds its achievement hollow, that having amassed black capital it does not know what to do with it, that success and prosperity seem transitory to this class and the cost too high? Do the members of this class ponder over the thought that human vanity does not survive the grave? This would be hard to believe.

Is the Communist class content? To say no would be to employ external, non-Soviet standards. This class has won in the game in which the whole nation is the loser. It must be considered fortunate, for otherwise one undermines faith in the Soviet regime, which gave the Communist class the most important of its blessings—power over the frightened, oppressed, humiliated, and degraded common man.

One final conclusion can be drawn from our analysis. To hope that a new generation of Communist partocrats capable of leading the regime toward liberalization will appear in the Soviet political arena is an illusion. Nothing fundamental can change in the communist system without destroying the system itself. If this occurs, it will be necessary to talk in terms of anti-Communist, not Communist, leaders.

Notes

1. Alexander Yanov, *Detente After Brezhnev: The Domestic Roots of Soviet Foreign Policy,* Policy Papers in International Affairs (Berkeley: Institute of International Studies, 1977), pp. 1–2.

2. M. Voslensky, *Nomenclatura* (in Russian) (London: Overseas Publications, 1984), pp. 283, 296, 299, 330–331.

Three Scenarios for the Possible Evolution of the Communist Class

Contradictions within the Communist class which were already noticeable in the 1970s became even more pronounced by the early 1980s. The ruling oligarchy has become more autarkic and has proved unwilling and unable to share its power with the elites who serve it: the bureaucratic, scientific, military, cultural-artistic, and other elites. It is now quite evident that the ruling oligarchy of the Communist class has been, for the seventy years of its hold on power, unable to fulfill any of its promises to the people: to raise the living standard of the population to Western levels or to guarantee the various Soviet nationalities democratic rights, equality, and freedom of development.

Consequently, the ruling oligarchy will be able to remain in power only under conditions of persisting opposition to (or, more accurately, struggle against) the elite by transforming the existing internal contradictions within the elite into external ones relating to the common people, who are equally hostile to all strata and groups of the Communist class. In this regard several scenarios are possible.

Scenario 1

The partocratic oligarchy will completely succeed in subordinating the Communist class to itself and in mobilizing it in order to perpetuate the totalitarian regime. In its struggle against the elite of the Communist class the partocratic oligarchy may even try to elicit support from some segments of the common populace by capitalizing on the latter's hostility and jealousy toward the "haves." A precedent was set in China in the 1960s when Mao used young people (the Red Guards) to partially crush and completely subjugate the partocracy. If this precedent is followed, the totalitarian regime in the Soviet Union will become even more severe than it is now. The iron curtain will slam down tight: cultural, scientific, and possibly also commercial ties with the free world will be severed. On the home front, the Communist class would be degraded, as in the 1930s and 1940s, to the social status of a bunch of elites completely dependent on and subordinate to the top authorities. On the spiritual plane, a siege-mentality psychology will be actively encouraged.

Although this is a possibility, the development of Soviet society in such a direction in the 1980s is not very likely, since it would require terror on Stalin's scale and a leader of Stalin's mold. Theoretically, such a development cannot be precluded: the very nature of the Soviet regime allows for the possibility, and even the necessity, of mass terror and deification of a leader. It must be remembered, however, that during the past twenty-five years the regime has not been working at "full capacity" and has been using only "selective" terror and leaders with diluted authority. However, although the regime has not really changed during this period, the elites have changed, for they have become a class that has tasted the pleasures of personal security, material comfort, privilege, and social prestige.

Scenario 2

The dependent elites of the Communist class could overthrow the currently ruling partocratic oligarchy but not make any social or political reforms. This is almost what happened under Andropov. It seemed as if the partocracy was about to be dethroned by the powerful KGB elite, but soon there would emerge from its midst just the same partocratic oligarchy or an oligarchy quite similar to the one that had been overthrown.

In that event, the contradiction between the Communist class and the ruling oligarchy would remain. The ensuing configuration of forces would determine policy: the new oligarchy might be inclined to share power with the elites because of its relative youth and lack of experience. In the process of its maturation and consolidation, however, the new oligarchy would have to bow to the inherent laws of development of communist society and attempt to effect a greater concentration and centralization of power, until the clash of interests and goals between the Communist class and the ruling oligarchy would lead to a renewed conflict. Then the explosion would occur so that the development of Soviet society would follow the first scenario.

Scenario 3

The Communist class would get rid of the oligarchy without creating a new one. Such an upheaval would lead to radical changes in the whole social structure of Soviet society, first in the structure of the Communist class itself. It would mark the end-point of its being a class in itself, but before this could happen the Communist class would make its rights and privileges hereditary. The official ideology of Soviet society as it now stands precludes this development for purely symbolic reasons, only because it continues to pay lip service to basic, pseudo-socialist principles which to a certain extent limit the rights (but not the status or power) of individuals and social groups.

In order to free itself from this ideologically imposed limitation, the Communist class needs an ally. Obviously unsuited for this role are the toiling masses, who want to eliminate rather than perpetuate existing social inequalities. In its search for allies, the Communist class will find a community of interest with a social group that has arisen in Soviet society outside the framework of the officially recognized stratification. This potential ally is made up of various groups of "operators" and all kinds of wheeler-dealers who have succeeded in amassing huge fortunes for themselves through the medium of the black market "second economy." They have what the Communist class needs—capital—whereas the Communist class has in abundance what the underground capitalists direly need to legitimize their social position—official recognition and status.

Cooperation between the Communist class and underground capitalists has been customary for a long time. Privileges have long been sold and status bought. More and more often, representatives of the Communist class are today being transformed from patrons or protectors of the "second economy" into its organizers and directors, while those active in the "second economy" are making their way into the Communist class, with the most dynamic of them even pushing into the ruling oligarchy.

Social mobility between the Communist class and the underground capitalists might finally lead to their merger, to the formation of a new ruling class whose domination would be ensured by inheritable capital, status, and privilege. At present the single remaining barrier to this development is the ideological framework of the Soviet state. Were this to collapse or be dismantled, as the increasingly disastrous shape of the communist economy might well necessitate, a completely new type of regime might well follow in the Soviet Union. Power would then be divided: governmental power would be in the hands of a political oligarchy—the successor to the Communist class—and managerial power would be wielded by an elite that emerged from the "second economy" businessmen.

It is difficult to predict the orientation of such a regime. A wide range of variations would then be possible: from a tendency toward isolationism (which is unlikely) to a much more probable collaboration with other classes of Soviet society. If this scenario materializes at all, it can be expected no sooner than the early twenty-first century, when the other scenarios (both those described above and others not considered here) have run their course or have failed.

In focusing on the Communist class, the scenarios presented here have intentionally ignored what is potentially the most decisive force in Soviet politics—the common people. Yet the social attitudes and political orientation of the masses can definitely alter significantly any scenario and create a variety of possibilities totally different from those considered above. Indeed, the Soviet masses may well succeed in directing or affecting developments in the USSR according to their own scenario, in other words, in simultaneously being authors, directors, and main dramatis personae of events of their own choosing.

Bibliography

Armstrong, John. *Ideology, Politics, and Government in the Soviet Union: An Introduction.* 3rd ed. London: Nelson, 1973.

Bergson, Abram, and Herbert S. Levine (eds.). *The Soviet Economy: Toward the Year 2000.* London: Allen and Unwin, 1983.

Bottomore, T. B. *Elites and Society.* Harmondsworth: Penguin, 1966.

Brown, A. H. *Soviet Politics and Political Science.* London: Macmillan, 1974.

Brown, Archie, and Michael Kaser (eds.). *Soviet Policy for the 1980s.* London: Macmillan, 1982.

Djilas, Milovan. *The New Class.* London: Allen and Unwin, 1966.

Dmytryshyn, Basil. *USSR: A Concise History.* 4th ed. New York: Charles Scribner's Sons, 1984.

George, V., and N. Manning. *Socialism, Social Welfare, and the Soviet Union.* London: Routledge and Keagan Paul, 1980.

Glezerman, G., and M. Iovchuk. "Soviet Way of Life, the Building of a New Man." *Kommunist* 4: 119–125.

Harasymiw, Bohdan. "*Nomenclatura:* The Soviet Communist Party's Leadership Recruitment System." *Canadian Journal of Political Science* 2: 493–512.

Heitlinger, A. *Women and State Socialism: Sex Inequality in the Soviet Union and Czechoslovakia.* London: Macmillan, 1979.

Hill, Ronald J., and Peter Frank. *The Soviet Communist Party.* 2nd ed. London: Allen and Unwin, 1983.

Hirszowicz, M. *The Bureaucratic Leviathan: A Study in the Sociology of Communism.* London: Martin Robertson, 1980.

Hough, Jerry F. *Soviet Leadership in Transition.* Washington, D.C.: The Brookings Institution, 1980.

Hough, Jerry F. *The Soviet Union and Social Science Theory.* Cambridge, Mass.: Harvard University Press, 1977.

Hough, Jerry F., and Merle Fainsod. *How the Soviet Union Is Governed.* Cambridge, Mass.: Harvard University Press, 1979.

Jacobs, E. M. "Urban Housing in the Soviet Union." In NATO Directorate of Economic Affairs, *Economic Aspects of Life in the USSR.* Brussels, 1975.

Kaser, Michael. *Health Care In the Soviet Union and Eastern Europe.* London: Croom Helm, 1976.

Keller, Suzanne. "Elites." In David L. Sills (ed.), *The International Encyclopedia of the Social Sciences* 15. New York: Macmillan and the Free Press, 1968, pp. 26–27.

Lane, David. *Politics and Society in the USSR.* 2nd ed. London: Martin Robertson, 1978.

Lane, David. *The Socialist Industrial State: Toward a Political Sociology of State Socialism.* London: Allen and Unwin, 1976.

Lapidus, Warshofsky Gail (ed.). *Women, Work, and Family in the Soviet Union.* Armonk, N.Y.: M. E. Sharpe, 1984.

Lewin, M. *Political Undercurrents in Soviet Economic Debates.* Princeton: Princeton University Press, 1974.

Littlejohn, Gary. *A Sociology of the Soviet Union.* New York: St. Martin's Press, 1984.

Matthews, Mervin. *Class and Society in Soviet Russia.* London: Allen Lane, 1972.

Matthews, Mervin. *Privilege in the Soviet Union: A Study of Elite Life-Styles Under Communism.* London: Allen and Unwin, 1978.

McAuley, A. *Economic Welfare in the Soviet Union.* Madison: University of Wisconsin Press, 1979.

Moses, Joel C. "The Impact of Nomenklatura in Soviet Regional Elite Recruitment." *Soviet Union* 8, part 1 (1981): 62–102.

Munting, Roger. *Economic Development of the USSR.* New York: St. Martin's Press, 1984.

NATO Directorate of Economic Affairs. *Economic Aspects of Life in the USSR.* Brussels, 1975.

Nove, Alec. "Is There a Ruling Class in the USSR?" *Soviet Studies* 27, no. 4 (October 1975): 615–638.

Pankhurst, J., and M. Sacks (eds.). *Contemporary Soviet Society: Sociological Perspectives.* New York: Praeger, 1980.

Parry, G. *Political Elites.* London: Allen and Unwin, 1969.

Rigby, T. H., Archie Brown, and Peter Reddaway. *Authority, Power and Policy in the USSR: Essays Dedicated to Leonard Schapiro.* London: Macmillan, 1980.

Rose, N. "Socialism and Social Policy: The Problems of Inequality." *Politics and Power* 2. London: Routledge and Keagan Paul, 1980.

Shakhnazarov, G. H. *Sotsialisticheskaya demokratiya, nekotorye voprosy teorii* (Socialist Democracy: Some Problems of Theory). Moscow: Politizdat, 1974.

Shatz, Marshall. *Stalin, the Great Purge, and Russian History: A New*

Look at the New Class. Carl Beck Paper in Russian and East European Studies, no. 305. Pittsburgh, Pa.: University of Pittsburgh.

Shipler, David K. *Russia: Broken Idols, Solemn Dreams.* New York: N.Y. Times Books, 1983, pp. 163–248.

Sotsialistichesky obraz zhizni i sovremennaya ideologicheskaya bor'ba (The Way of Life Under Socialism and the Contemporary Ideological Struggle). Moscow: Politizdat, 1976.

White, Stephen, John Gardner, and George Schopflin. *Communist Political Systems.* New York: St. Martin's Press, 1984.

Zemtsov, Ilya. *La corruption en Union Sovietique* (Corruption in the Soviet Union). Paris: Hachette, 1976.